ART AT THE SPEED OF LIFE

motivation + inspiration for making mixed-media art every day

pam carriker

 INTERWEAVE.
interweave.com

Editor	Elaine Lipson
Art Director	Liz Quan
Designer	Lee Calderon
Photography	Brad Bartholomew
Illustration	Ann Sabin Swanson
Production	Katherine Jackson

Interweave Press LLC
201 East Fourth Street
Loveland, CO 80537
interweave.com

Printed in China by Asia Pacific Offset Ltd.

Library of Congress Cataloging-in-Publication Data

Art at the speed of life : motivation and inspiration for making
mixed-media art every day / [Pam Carriker ... et al.].
   p. cm.
 Includes bibliographical references and index.
ISBN 978-1-59668-491-1 (eBook)
ISBN 978-1-59668-261-0 (pbk.)
1. Handicraft. 2. Art--Technique. I. Carriker, Pam.
TT857.A78 2010
745.5--dc22
                     2010035434

10 9 8 7 6 5 4 3 2 1

ACKNOWLEDGMENTS

I have to admit that I thought about what I would write and who I'd thank for helping me bring this book to life long before it got to this point. Now that I'm here I realize just how many people it takes to make a book!

First it takes someone believing in you, someone who gives you wings and teaches you to fly. Being married to a pilot with a flight instructor's permit comes in handy for that! To my dearest husband, Nathan, more thanks than I can possibly voice, from the depths of my heart.

To my three wonderful boys—all right, one boy and two men—you are my inspiration. As I watch you grow and try to manage our home, I've realized how quickly time flies by. You teach me every day to appreciate the ordinary and revel in the extraordinary. Watching you spread your wings gives me the courage to spread my own.

Most people have two parents, but I've been blessed with four. As far back as I can remember each has encouraged me on my artistic journey. You've always been there for me, and not one of you has ever seemed as surprised as I am at the artful blessings that have come my way. To my extended family, sister, brothers, and in-laws, you're always there right when I need you, and I so appreciate that.

To all of my artist friends who contributed their amazing talents to this book, I thank each and every one of you. I was told that trying to get this many artists to meet deadlines would be like herding cats—well, let me just say that you all are the cat's meow!

I want to thank the team at Interweave, and in particular my editor Elaine Lipson for her patience at showing a new author the ropes. She helped me to see the light at the end of the tunnel, and her attention to detail helped make this book what it is. The lessons I've learned will stay with me a lifetime. Many thanks to Pokey Bolton and Tricia Waddell for believing in this book from the beginning and encouraging me to keep trying.

Finally, I must give thanks to the "Master Artist" for putting these people in my life, this dream in my heart, and the brush in my hand.

CONTENTS

LIVING THE ARTFUL LIFE

The idea for this book started as a small seed—actually, as my very first article. I remember vividly the conversation going on inside my head. One side of my brain was jumping up and down and the other was wondering what I'd gotten myself into. As that seed was watered with the encouragement of my amazing husband and artist friends, it began to grow roots. I started to wonder, "Why can't I do this?" instead of "What are you thinking?"

My journey into publishing started with a desire to share my ideas about fitting art into a busy life. As I created this book I often had to stop and take my own advice or that of one of the contributors. I truly practice what I preach. As leaves branched out of the seedling that grew bigger and stronger each day, and as the plant grew, so did I. I learned that if you put fear aside you can do many things. I also learned that no one's perfect, and we all bring our special gifts to the table.

FROM SEED
TO BLOSSOM

Art doesn't always just happen. It's a great thing when it does, and the moment should be treasured, but many of us have to plan for it and fit it into the tightly woven schedules of busy lives. If you forget to water your creative spirit every day, it can begin to shrivel just as a new plant will. Your spirit thrives when the right amount of attention is given to it and so does creativity.

Just when you start to wonder whether all of the planning and juggling are worth it, you look at your plant and see a bud—the promise of a future bloom! Maybe someone wants to buy a piece of your work, or an art magazine wants to publish your work. That bud then becomes your focus as you wait with expectation for it to bloom. When that happens, you'll know without a doubt that you are living an artful life. Others will see it, too, and will be encouraged on their own journey. Creating art is not just about you. It's about all of us on the path to living art at the speed of life.

ABOUT THIS
BOOK

This book is a tool to access all parts of your creativity, bringing them together to become the art-filled life of your dreams. In each chapter, you'll find an *Artist Spotlight* project from a talented contributor. From textured backgrounds and collage to assemblage and encaustics, from paper clay to mixed-media portraits, the projects provide a multitude of techniques for you to explore. I then offer a second *Speed of Life* project in each chapter, inspired by the Spotlight project but geared to creating a similar work of art in less time. This hands-on approach, along with tips from the contributors and essays focused on leading a productive, creative life, will help you on your artful journey.

Chapter 1 includes instructions for an easy handmade journal (page 24), and at the end of each chapter, you'll find ideas for adding to that journal. Through this *Seven-Day Journal* project, you'll discover how easy it can be to keep an art journal and get in the habit of creating every day. By the end of this book you will have completed multiple backgrounds, many finished pieces of art, and a complete art journal. You'll be well on the way to establishing a creative habit that leads to living art at the speed of life.

Art Credits: page 143

I WANT TO BE AN ARTIST WHEN I GROW UP!

Being an artist doesn't have to remain a child-hood dream. Despite your grown-up obligations, there's a child inside of you who desperately wants to be an artist, too. Many people enjoy the best of both worlds, and with a little change of mindset, you can, too. I always wanted to be an artist, but fast approaching age forty, I was afraid it wasn't attainable, not as a real job. Being artsy-craftsy is one thing, I thought, but being an artist? That was on another level completely. Yet with determination, I finally began to achieve my dream of becoming an artist while also living a busy, demanding life. I developed a lot of tricks along the way that I will share with you.

In this chapter, we will begin the journey to make the most of our creative time by creating multiple backgrounds at one time. These backgrounds will be used throughout the following chapters to complete the *Speed of Life* projects. In this chapter's *Artist Spotlight* project, Christy Hydeck peels back the layers of how she creates her richly textured pieces of art, and my *Speed of Life* version shows how to make a supply of backgrounds to work with. I'll also show you how to quickly create your own handmade art journal from your favorite paper; use it for the *Seven-Day Journal* project that runs throughout the book.

Art Credits: page 143

enjoy lifes simple pleasures

THE MULTIPLE-PROJECTS RULE

Finding time to be creative is something that you may struggle with, leading to frustration that stifles your muse before you even get started. I've got a tip that's a big time-saver. It takes virtually no extra time to prep two substrates (surfaces for painting and collage) if you are going to prep one. Now multiply that by ten—why not prepare ten substrates at a time?

I know, it seems like a lot to manage at one time, but if you're going to get out the gesso and dirty a brush, then learn from Henry Ford and start an assembly line; you'll thank yourself later. Having a stack of prepped substrates gets you one step closer to having a stack of finished artwork.

We'll apply this principle of doing more than one piece at a time throughout the book. It's part of a change in your mind-set that will help you to make more art. Each time you reach for an art product; ask yourself, "Can I use this on something else while I have it out?" Dirty your tools once, do multiple projects, clean up once, and save yourself valuable time and effort. You get the messy work done in one fell swoop and set yourself up to be successful. Think multitasking versus individual projects. When you work on a variety of pieces this way, you can sandwich more frequent art time into your day.

> **THINK MULTITASKING VERSUS INDIVIDUAL PROJECTS.**

It's also helpful to work on several pieces in different stages of completion, working on less messy techniques one time and getting out the paint and brushes another. It'll enable you to pick and choose the medium you feel like working with or the project you're inspired to work on at any given time.

Pam Carriker, *Simple Pleasures*.
8" × 10" (20.5 × 25.5 cm). Mixed-media collage with paint, water-soluble crayon, and graphite pencil.

STAYING YOUNG AT ART

by Suzi Blu

Suzi Blu, *A Lovely Dream*. 7" × 9" (18 × 23 cm). Mixed-media art journal.

Are you an artist? Maybe you believe that you can't be an artist because you can't draw portraits, aren't in a gallery, didn't graduate from art school, or haven't sold your work. That's a lot of pressure for little ol' you, sitting down with your sketchbook just wanting to draw something pretty. I believe it is passion, not a degree, that makes you an artist. It is your excitement about materials, colors, and textures, your enthusiasm when you see work you like and ooh, you want to run home and do it, too. This makes you an artist.

It is a fallacy that artists are born. Artists work hard to master their craft. On the gallery walls, you don't see all the preliminary sketches and canvases that were screwed up before the artist got it right. The only difference between you and an art master is time. Gaining skills is a wonderful goal, but respect wherever you are on the art path. By creating, you are manifesting something where nothing existed, and this in itself is amazing. You are a little god, creator of your own universe, so any mark you make is sacred. Remember that.

Even when they have never painted before, children possess confidence and freedom with art. There is no, "What if red ruins the painting?" Or, "I'm not as good as Sally so I shouldn't even try." Children know what art school graduates have forgotten: that everything they make is beautiful.

I long to paint with the bravado of a child despite years of art-school training. I can draw realistically but find great joy in a simplistic form. I paint folk art and I'm proud of it. Not much in my paintings is in proportion; my art is raw, colorful, and full of life. Will my folk art be in museums? Probably not. Will it make people happy? Yes. Does it make me happy? YES! And for me, happy is more important than impressive.

INSPIRATION AT EVERY TURN

by Julie Bergmann

I find that inspiration can be both abundant and nonexistent. When I have the most time to work, I am not inspired, and when I have no time, I can think of dozens of things to create. Knowing how difficult it can be to find inspiration, I've learned to constantly view my surroundings and the world as potential contributors to my next piece.

When I began to explore new art media, my virtual instructors were the artists I admired, and I was replicating their work. It wasn't until I discovered papier-mâché as a sculpting medium that I saw my work begin to evolve into a style all its own. At that point, I was on my own. Fortunately, my muse was working overtime, and I found ideas for new pieces every day.

I found inspiration at every turn, in memories of my past and in my dreams of the future, in what was growing in my garden, in the words of my children, and my love for my family. I was soon submitting my works to publications, and some were accepted by the very publications that had previously inspired me. Then a publication invited me to share my techniques with other artists, and I became the artist who was inspiring others. "Talent is always conscious of its own abundance," said Alexander Solzhenitsyn, "and does not object to sharing." I love it when other artists share a technique of theirs with me, and I love to return the favor and pay it forward.

Today, when seeking inspiration for my art, I find it easiest when I don't try too hard. Just look around you and open your eyes to what is going on in your life. Inspiration is not always found in happiness; it can be a way to deal with difficult times as well. Creating a piece that expresses your feelings, good or bad, can be great therapy. Share your art with the world so others may be inspired as well.

Julie Bergmann, *The Man In The Moon*. 7" × 7" (18 × 18 cm). PaperClay.

REDEFINING THE BLANK CANVAS

by Christy Hydeck

MATERIALS

- Gel medium
- Canvas
- Assorted paper scraps and ephemera
- Tissue paper (white or colors)
- Modeling paste
- Acrylic satin-finish glazing liquid
- Acrylic paint: Naples yellow, titan buff, burnt sienna, burnt umber, white, blue, red
- Off-white crackle paint (I used Ranger Distress Crackle Paint in Old Paper)
- Skeleton leaves
- Gesso
- Graphite pencil
- Gold metallic paint
- Old sewing patterns
- Acrylic ink: black
- Gel pen: white

TOOLS

- Assorted paintbrushes, including a "scruffy" brush
- Stencil with your choice of design
- Metal spatula or palette knife
- Painting palette or small containers for mixing paint
- Heat gun
- Scrap pieces of bubble wrap 3" × 3" (7.5 × 7.5 cm)
- Brayer
- Baby wipes
- Awl, screwdriver, or other sharp object
- Old credit card
- Sanding block
- Waxed paper
- Blending stump
- Old toothbrush
- Calligraphy pen

This multilayered project makes the most of rich background layers. The beauty of this project lies in its secret basecoat of paper scraps, ephemera, and textural goodies. Select random pieces of paper in an assortment of colors and designs or personal ephemera such as receipts, ticket stubs, or portions of a handwritten note. Make sure they aren't precious to you, because those in the first layers may not show in the finished piece. Work loose and fast; go with your gut and fully immerse yourself in the process. Use this process to make backgrounds that can be the basis for many different kinds of finished work.

Christy Hydeck, *A Garden of Beautiful Deeds.*
16" × 20" (40.5 × 51 cm). Mixed-media collage with acrylic paint, papers, and ephemera.

FIG. 1

FIG. 2

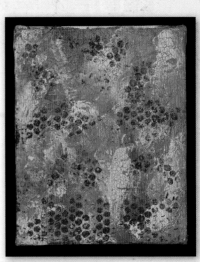

FIG. 3

1 Glue paper scraps onto the substrate with gel medium, overlapping to cover the canvas. When dry, add another layer of gel medium, laying tissue paper on top and covering with an additional layer of gel medium. Let the tissue wrinkle and rip.

2 Lay your stencil over part of the canvas. Using the metal spatula or palette knife, spread a thick coat of modeling paste over the stencil. Carefully lift the stencil straight up and flip it over to transfer the remaining modeling paste to the canvas to add texture. Let dry (**Figure 1**).

3 Drizzle glazing liquid over the canvas. Use a brush to scour Naples yellow paint on the canvas.

4 Mix one part glaze with two parts acrylic paint in red, yellow, and blue. Lightly brush a stripe of each color onto canvas, repeating colors as necessary. Load brush and pull down so the stripes fade toward the bottom and let the colors overlap. Let dry (**Figure 2**).

5 Randomly brush thick globs of crackle paint over the canvas. Brush out edges. Initiate crackling with a heat gun. Randomly stamp titan buff and burnt sienna paint on the canvas, using bubble wrap as a stamp (**Figure 3**).

6 Use an awl or a screwdriver tip to tear up some of the top layers and peel the paper back. Glue down loose pieces with gel medium and let dry.

7 Use gel medium to adhere a few skeleton leaves and use a credit card to scrape Naples yellow paint over the leaves. Let dry (**Figure 4**).

8 Lightly sand the entire canvas, varying the pressure for authentic aged results. Wipe off dust with a baby wipe. Add ephemera using gel medium to adhere. Paint glazing medium over the ephemera to incorporate it into the background; let dry (**Figure 5**).

9 Spread equal parts glazing medium and burnt sienna paint over a sheet of waxed paper and doodle a design with your awl or another sharp object. Transfer the design to your canvas by placing the

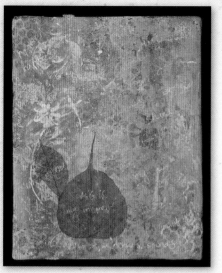

FIG. 4

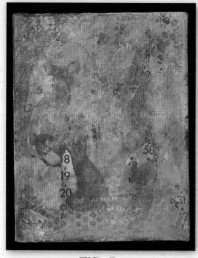

FIG. 5

FIG. 6

wet paint side on the canvas and burnishing. Peel waxed paper back and repeat. With a baby wipe, wipe away some of the design. Let dry. Brush a thin coat of gesso over the entire canvas. Let dry.

10 Use a graphite pencil to draw simple designs onto the canvas. Use a blending stump or your finger to smudge the pencil and work it into the canvas (**Figure 6**). Dry-brush metallic paint over the canvas to accentuate the texture.

11 Write words on torn pieces of a sewing pattern with pencil. Apply gel medium under and over the pattern pieces and place them on the canvas. Load an old toothbrush with diluted paint and run your finger over it to create a splatter on the canvas. Let dry.

12 Lightly sand your entire piece, sanding more heavily on the raised areas. Wipe off remaining sanding dust before proceeding.

13 Dip a calligraphy pen into the black acrylic ink and loosely outline your sketch. Add handwriting or a border with white gel pen to tie it all in.

BECOMING AN ARTIST AS A SECOND CAREER

by Jodi Ohl

Jodi Ohl, *New Beginning*. 6" × 12" (15 × 30.5 cm). Collage with acrylic paint on canvas.

day-to-day home and work activities. Fast-forward to my mid-thirties: I really needed to do something creative.

I started with watercolors and then began to dabble in collage and painting mediums. With each project I completed, I not only felt better emotionally, but I could also see my work improve. I started a blog to document my journey as a born-again artist. My readers cheered me on with every show-and-tell artwork I submitted to them.

It took fifteen years to find my way back to a creative life. Why? Because I feared I'd never be good enough. My blog readers and family believed in me as I started to showcase my art; in fact, one of my blog readers was my first buyer. Then I sold another piece. Soon I was motivated to continue because I felt nourished and accepted, and working on my art never seems like work; it is joyous, gratifying, illuminating, and fun. I learned that things happen when you need them to. I've also realized that we don't have to go down just one road in life. I don't have to give up being a mother, a banker, or a friend in order to pursue my artistic career.

As a child, did you dream you could be anything you wanted to be? I wanted to be a writer. I saw myself traveling the world, sitting in quaint cafes, working late into the night penning my adventures. Sweet dreams! Although I did earn an English degree, I excelled in business, so I took the safe and secure road. I was afraid of pursuing my dreams, so I did what I did well, instead of working hard to do what I loved. During the next phase of my life, I rarely wrote except in my journal. Life happened. I had little time for writing, art, or anything other than

My art career gives me the confidence to do something that was never a sure thing. It gives me joy, a vehicle to heal, and a chance to grow my wings. For now, I think things have worked out perfectly!

A CHANGE OF ART

If you find yourself throwing roadblocks in your own path, listing myriad reasons why you can't make art, try switching your thinking and listing the things you can do to enjoy a creative life. It can be as simple as a quick napkin sketch capturing that fleeting inspiration or a layer of paint added to a canvas. Even checking off household chores on your to-do list paves the way for creative time in the near future, so let the anticipation of art time build while completing the necessary daily tasks. Visualize the reward of creating art as you work through your day. Every small step leads you further down the path to leading a more fulfilling, creative life.

The instructions on page 21 guide you in making several backgrounds at once, so they'll be ready for everything from journal pages to canvas work whenever you have even a few spare minutes. This will go a long way toward setting up a productive work environment and helping you to utilize the small windows of creative time as they become available. Admire your handiwork and pat yourself on the back for this major step!

Pam Carriker, *A Change of Heart*. 8" × 8" (20.5 × 20.5 cm). Mixed-media collage with acrylic paints.

THERE IS NO GREATER HARM THAN THAT OF WASTED TIME.
—MICHELANGELO

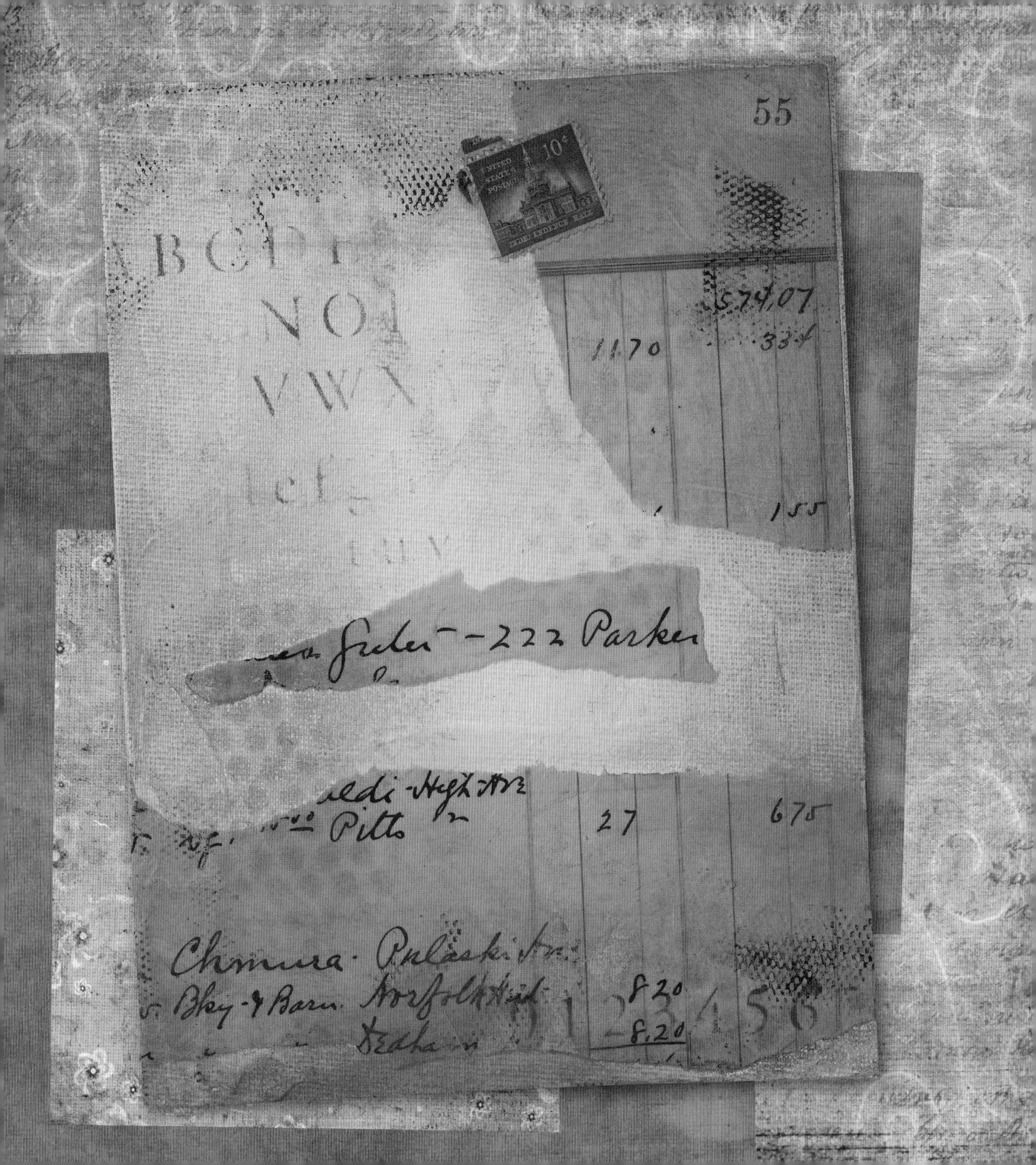

55

UNITED STATES POSTAGE 10¢ INDEPENDENCE HALL

A B C D E
N O
V W X
letg
tuv

$74.07
1170   33 4

155

Fuler - 222 Parker

ldi High #2
Pitts   27   675

Chmura · Pulaski St.
Bkg & Barn. Norfolk #...
Graham   8.20
                        -8.20
1 2 3 4 5 6

CREATING MULTIPLE BACKGROUNDS

Creating multiple backgrounds, each one ready for further treatment, allows you to come back to your art when you have only a small window of time. By adding collage elements, fabric, paint, or writing, you can turn prepared backgrounds into finished works of art in short order. By creating several backgrounds at once, you make it easy to work in series with pieces tied together by color and texture. The idea is simple: use your tools to do as many things as you can while you have them out and clean up one time.

MATERIALS

- A variety of substrates, such as canvas, artist panel, cradled hardboard, and watercolor paper
- Gesso
- Acrylic paints: heavy-body titanium white, hansa yellow light, fluid nickel azo gold, fluid transparent yellow iron oxide, fluid cobalt teal, raw umber, coarse iridescent stainless steel, any dark color
- Collage scraps and vintage papers
- Soft gel medium
- Graphite pencil
- Satin acrylic glazing medium
- Permanent inkpads
- Texturing materials such as sequin waste
- Satin-finish glazing medium

TOOLS

- 2" (5 cm) chip brush or sponge brush
- Palette knife (optional)
- Brayer
- Baby wipes
- Texturing tools such as rubber stamps, sponges, plastic bags, Legos
- Old toothbrush

Pam Carriker, *Prepared Background*. 5" × 7" (12.5 × 18 cm). Mixed media on canvas board.

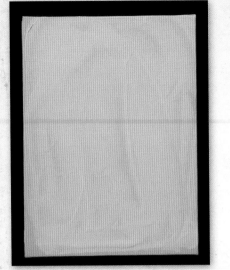

FIG. 1

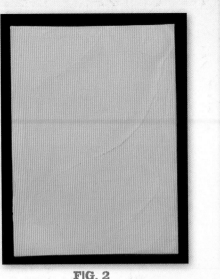

FIG. 2

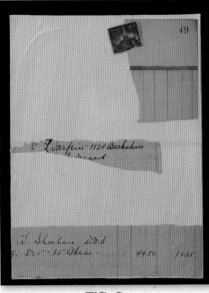

FIG. 3

GRUNGY GLAZE RECIPE

Applying this glaze over your background will knock down bright colors and give an aged appearance to the work. Just mix the following ingredients together and apply to your project with a wide brush going in one direction. You can substitute any coarse metallic paint for the iridescent stainless steel paint to create different looks.

- 3 tablespoons satin glazing medium
- 3 or 4 drops raw umber fluid acrylic paint
- 1 drop nickel azo gold fluid acrylic paint
- 1 drop Golden Paints coarse iridescent stainless steel paint

1 Lay out your substrates on a large worktable or counter. Use a variety of substrates so you'll have many choices for later projects. Coat all substrates with gesso, using a large 2" (5 cm) sponge or chip brush. Make your brush strokes random or try trowling the gesso on with a palette knife for a smoother texture. Let dry thoroughly **(Figure 1)**.

2 Paint a base coat on all substrates with a light yellow color. I use a mixture of Golden brand paints in heavy-body titanium white, hansa yellow light, and a couple of drops of fluid nickel azo gold **(Figure 2)**.

3 Adhere collage papers if desired. I usually add collage elements in the form of vintage papers to some of the substrates and leave others plain. Using soft gel medium and a wide sponge or chip brush, coat the back of the paper first and then apply some medium to the substrate. Lay the collage paper on the wet substrate and gently pat into place. Use a brayer to ensure good contact with the substrate. Take the time to work out any bubbles so your end product is nice and smooth **(Figure 3)**.

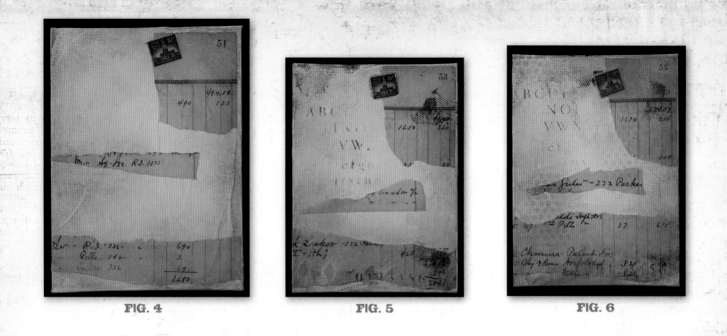

FIG. 4   FIG. 5   FIG. 6

4 Add fluid transparent yellow iron oxide to the edges of the substrates and blend in toward the center, being careful not to cover over the entire undercoat. Use a baby wipe for easy blending or feather the color in with the sponge brush or chip brush. Let dry **(Figure 4)**.

5 Follow with a layer of fluid nickel azo gold color applied in the same way. If you don't have text in your collage items, add your own writing using a graphite pencil or stamp some text with ink and a rubber stamp **(Figure 5)**.

6 Create texture with sequin waste, stamping, stencils, bubble wrap, a sea sponge, a plastic bag, Legos, or really just about anything. Using leftover paint on your palette, gesso, or an inkpad, stamp or stencil randomly onto your background. Don't overdo it; use hints of texture here and there **(Figure 6)**.

7 Using full-strength fluid acrylic paint in teal and a baby wipe, add color and more textural interest in three spots on each substrate.

8 If desired, using the wide chip or sponge brush, apply Grungy Glaze (see opposite) to all substrates, going in the same direction from top to bottom. Leave brushstrokes in or use a baby wipe to remove and blend as needed. This step knocks down the colors a bit for a vintage, aged look.

9 If desired, using any dark color of acrylic paint, add water and mix to an inky consistency. With an old toothbrush, pick up some of the paint and run your thumb across the bristles to spatter small specks of paint. It's a good idea to test it on your palette first before doing it on your artwork. This "fly specking" technique adds texture and depth. The paint will splatter, so be sure to protect walls and surfaces around you.

TEN-MINUTE JOURNAL

If you're not already keeping an art journal, now is the time to start. I create backgrounds and add layers to journal pages while working on other projects. Think of your art as the smaller parts of a larger whole; all of the pieces work together. A journal is a reflection of your creative self and the work you're doing, not a separate project. Creating your own handmade journal cuts down on the expense of purchasing a readymade journal, and it gives you one more way to create something personal and unique. My method gives you a handbound look quickly and easily.

TIPS

- To make a different-size journal, start with a different-size paper. You can vary the page size within the journal by not folding into equal thirds in the first step. For a thicker journal, make several of the journals described above and stitch together.

- Pages may curl initially if you use wet media, but painting both sides will help them lay flat. Put the journal under a heavy book overnight to flatten it.

Above: Ten-Minute Journal with blank pages ready to paint.

Top, left: Ten-Minute Journal with painted cover and attached button for closure.

MATERIALS

- One sheet watercolor paper, 22" × 30" (56 × 76 cm)
- Waxed linen thread
- Beads, buttons, or trinkets (optional)

Finished size: 8" × 8" (20.5 × 20.5 cm) journal with twelve two-sided pages

TOOLS

- Bone folder
- Awl or sharp needle
- Large needle such as a yarn darner

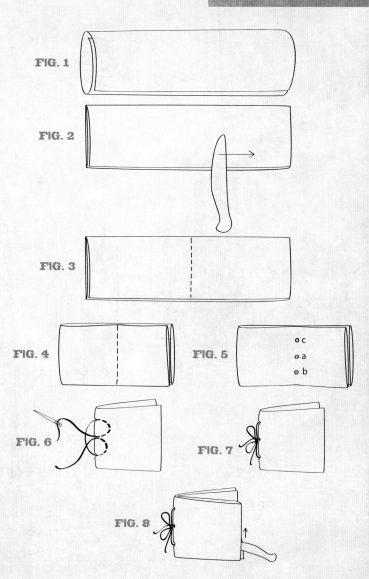

FIG. 1

FIG. 2

FIG. 3

FIG. 4

FIG. 5

o c
o a
o b

FIG. 6

FIG. 7

FIG. 8

1 Lay the sheet of paper on a counter, in horizontal orientation. Loosely roll the paper from the bottom to the top so it's divided into thirds (**Figure 1**).

2 Flatten and press the folds with the bone folder (**Figure 2**).

3 Keeping the paper in horizontal orientation, fold in half, left to right (**Figure 3**). Press the fold with the bone folder.

4 Fold in half left to right one more time and again press the fold with the bone folder (**Figure 4**).

5 Open the book and lay flat. Using the awl, poke three holes into the inside fold/spine of the book (**Figure 5**). One hole should be in the middle and the other two about 1½" (3.8 cm) from the top and bottom.

6 Measure a length of waxed thread by doubling the width of the open journal. Thread the needle and go through the middle hole (a) on the outside of the journal leaving a tail of about 6" (15 cm). Go through the bottom hole (b) on the inside running the thread up the back of the journal and into the top hole (c) (**Figure 6**).

7 Go through the inside middle hole and tie the two ends together around the outside long stitch (**Figure 7**).

8 Wet a paintbrush or your finger with some water and run it on all of the folds of the pages except the spine. You'll have to wet your finger several times.

Place the bone folder inside a fold and gently rip the fold open as if you were opening a letter with a letter opener. Do this to all folds except the spine (**Figure 8**).

9 Add beads, buttons, or trinkets to the strings, if desired.

SEVEN-DAY JOURNAL
DAY 1: GETTING STARTED

Each chapter of this book includes instructions for adding to the handmade Ten-Minute Journal (page 24). When you've worked through all the instructions, you'll have seven wonderful sets of pages in your art journal and a good start on a creative habit you can take with you anywhere. It's so easy to add to pages that already have color and texture. Having many pages in varying stages of completion helps let go of the need to create a perfect page from start to finish.

MATERIALS

- Acrylic paint (use leftover paint on your palette from other projects)
- 2" (5 cm) chip brush or sponge brush
- Glazing medium
- Permanent inkpad in black or brown
- Graphite pencil

TOOLS

- 2" (5 cm) chip brush or sponge brush
- Rubber stamps

1 As you use each paint color on substrates for the projects in this chapter, take the leftover paint and thin it down with water and a bit of acrylic glazing medium. Use a ratio of one part liquid acrylic paint and one part water, with a small amount of acrylic glazing medium, to create a wash of color. Use the thinned paint on a whole page or partial page and do as many pages as you can until the paint runs out.

2 Continue this process with each color of paint you use on your projects. Jump around in your journal to vary the color of your pages. Let the paint dry between layers so your colors stay true and don't get muddy.

3 When you use a stamp or other tool in a project, use it again in your journal before you clean it up. If it's already out and dirty, use it again before you clean it up.

4 Do some writing on your pages. Using a graphite pencil, write out your feelings. They will end up mostly covered as you add to the journal, so don't worry about what you write at this stage.

TIPS

- Try painting the watercolor paper, front and back, before folding it into the journal—you'll never worry about starting on a blank page!

- For a sturdier cover, paint the outside and inside of the front and back pages with gesso before adding paint or cut chipboard to size and glue to the front and back with craft glue. Paint the chipboard with gesso, let dry, and add paint.

- Keep your journal at the ready while you work on multiple backgrounds (page 21). Use up the leftover paint on your palette by watering it down and painting several pages in your journal. Use a baby wipe to blend the paint quickly and save the used wipes to add to the pages as collage elements later.

Pam Carriker, *Seven-Day Journal*. 8" × 8" (20.5 × 20.5 cm) closed. Handmade journal with mixed-media pages.

CHAPTER 2

SO MANY SUPPLIES
SO LITTLE TIME

IT'S IMPORTANT TO FOCUS ON THE METHODS AND MEDIA YOU REALLY LOVE, AND RESIST THE TEMPTATION TO TRY EVERY NEW THING THAT COMES OUT.

Who hasn't gone to the art supply store to replace a must-have jar of medium that's just run dry, only to walk out with bulging bags and an empty wallet, unable to resist all those luscious colors of paint and paper? It makes you want to try any and everything! Yet coming home to an already overcrowded studio to try to find a place for those purchases can be frustrating. Having too many materials can stifle creativity, working against you. It's important to focus on the methods and media you really love and resist the temptation to try every new thing that comes out.

This chapter will help you sharpen your focus and make the most of fewer supplies. The *Artist Spotlight* project by Brandie Butcher-Isley uses old family photos to tell the stories of people from days gone by. In my *Speed of Life* variation, you'll tackle clutter and get down to the business of making art using one of the backgrounds prepared in chapter one to create a vintage-look collage with a modern photo. Collage is a great way to use and reuse scraps of papers and things that otherwise might be discarded, so add some of those scraps to your journal as you continue on the *Seven-Day Journal* project.

Art Credits: page 143

PYRAMID
SCHEMING

Take a few minutes to answer a few simple questions and get a game plan together to help you be successful in your pursuit of Art. This is a great little journal exercise you'll be able to refer to when the supply fairies start calling to you! First, draw a pyramid of lines in your journal, as shown below.

1 On the top line, list your favorite type of art (such as collage, painting, drawing, assemblage).

2 On the second line, list your two favorite media to work with (such as paint, pastels, paper, rusty findings).

3 On the third line, list three to five complementary media that enhance your primary two media (such as colored pencils, charcoal, rubber stamps, water-soluble crayon, stencils).

4 On the bottom line, list the types of art can you make from the supplies you've listed.

Even with a narrowed focus on just a few media, you can create a lot of art. You really don't need to have every single art supply that's available.

So what do you do with all of the excess supplies that build up over time?

FOCUSING ON WHAT YOU LOVE BEST AND UNCLUTTERING YOUR MIND AND YOUR STUDIO SPACE ARE CRUCIAL TO PRODUCING MORE ARTWORK.

De-stash: Verb meaning to give away or sell unused artsy treasures to other artists, as in "I'm de-stashing my excess vintage papers, anyone want some?" Often used on selling sites in conjunction with selling artwork.

Although it can be hard to part with some of your treasures, the benefits far outweigh the negatives. More work room, a clear focus, and the joy of sharing with others are just a few of the positive things that come from de-stashing.

_____
Favorite type of art

_____ _____
Favorite two media

_____ _____ _____
Additional complementary media

_____ _____ _____ _____
What can you do with just these supplies?

KEEPING ART AFFORDABLE

In tough economic times, things like buying or creating art often end up on the back burner. The challenges of managing a household, the ever-increasing cost of living, and the need to be frugal don't diminish your need to create. Here are some simple money-saving strategies.

1 *Use supplies you already have on hand.* Look through your work space for any supplies you purchased and haven't used yet. We get excited about a new technique or product, rush out to buy it, and then it sits in our studio gathering dust. Use it, trade it with a friend, or sell it online.

Pam Carriker, *Be Still.* 8" × 8" (20.5 × 20.5 cm). Mixed media with vintage papers, acrylic paints, and Liquid Pencil on hardboard.

2 *Finish projects you started and never finished.* Go through your unfinished projects and set a time to finish them; if you've lost interest, recycle or appropriately discard the materials. Unfinished projects weigh on your spirit and take up space.

3 *Save leftover paint and scraps of paper.* Use leftovers in your art journal, make a card, or create some mail art to submit to a magazine for publication. Organize scraps by color in see-through drawers. Host a scrap swap on your blog.

4 *Host an art swap.* Swapping art with friends is a fun way to collect and share art with others, as well as lift each other's spirits. Who doesn't love a good mail day? It's becoming increasingly rare to get a letter, card, or package in the mail, and nothing brightens your day more. Pay it forward!

5 *Reinvent older works.* Take work that didn't sell and make it into something new! Collage right over it or cut the canvas off the frame and make it the cover for your next art journal. Art is meant to be seen, so get it out of hiding and give it new life.

6 *Become a coupon clipper.* Many craft/hobby stores offer online coupons, so take advantage of them. The two major stores in my area will allow you to use one coupon per day, so if I need a lot of things, I'll go back every day.

THE NEED TO BE FRUGAL DOESN'T DIMINISH YOUR NEED TO CREATE.

ARTIST ATTENTION DIVERSION DISORDER

by Cate Coulacos Prato

I can no longer hide the truth: I have AADD, or Artist Attention Diversion Disorder. You won't find this disorder in a psychiatry reference guide, but it exists. AADD is the curse of anyone whose mantra is, "So many supplies, so little time . . . oh look, there's something new I have to try!"

This is even more shameful because one of my jobs as former editor of *Cloth Paper Scissors Studios* magazine was to help people bring order—or at least some functionality—to their creative space. Often, the solution is for an artist to part with the fabrics, papers, and art supplies that haven't been used in years and critically assess whether they really need new products.

For me, it would be easier to have a functional studio if I limited myself to one or two media—knitting and painting, for example. But my AADD has me enthralled with collage for weeks, only to be mesmerized by beads. Then I read an article about felting, and it's off to buy dyed wool, needles, and felt balls. My fabric stash will come in handy when I start to make fabric books, but first I have to make some space for my fluid acrylics and that indigo dye kit that I got for Christmas.

I know that the solution isn't to "cure" my AADD, but to manage it. I've got some ideas of how to organize my space and make it work for me, and I'm delighted to pass these tips on to you.

1 *Fit the organization and storage to your style.* I work intensely on a project or in a medium for a while, and then I don't pick it up again for weeks or months, so I don't need all my supplies available at all times. Assigning a different bin or tray to knitting, paint supplies, jewelry making, stamping, etc., lets me take the supplies out when needed.

AADD

WHERE THE SPIRIT DOES NOT WORK
WITH THE HAND, THERE IS NO ART.
—LEONARDO DA VINCI

2 *Display some of your stash as collections.* I love to collect fabrics, trims, papers, and found objects. Some of these can be displayed. Think clear jars of buttons, framed pieces of fabrics, and so on.

3 *Keep frequently used supplies easy to reach.* I keep the supplies I use often—such as embroidery threads and needles, gel medium, decoupage medium, lace, and old denim—handy and near my worktable.

4 *Use labels and see-through storage.* I've spent too much time opening one opaque bin after another in search of that piece of chenille fabric I bought at a flea market two years ago. Labels and clear storage boxes make a big difference. And put things away as you go!

> LABELS AND CLEAR STORAGE BOXES MAKE A BIG DIFFERENCE.

5 *Don't bring it in the house.* Once you get known as a person who, for example, collects vintage fabrics, people start to say, "My Aunt Sarah just died and she has these wonderful old embroidered tablecloths. Would you like to look at them?" Well, yes, of course. But that doesn't mean you have to take them . . . at least not all of them.

6 *Make your work space a place you want to spend time in.* A cozy chair, colors you like, a safe place to rest a cup of coffee—maybe even bring in a small TV and DVD player. Then, instead of a mess, it will be a place to de-stress.

Julie Bergmann, *Sculpting a Dream.*
3" × 4½" × 3" (7.5 × 11.5 × 7.5 cm). Styrofoam, CelluClay, and mixed media.

LIVING ARTFULLY

by Suzan Buckner

I don't have trouble fitting art into my life; it's quite the other way around. I have to fit my life into my art. For example, I make a conscious decision to choose art over household chores. Only you can decide what to let go of and what has to be done, but once you draw that line, put all of your energy into it! There's no point in wasting time dwelling on those lesser important tasks.

Boredom is a constant battle for me. I have always had problems keeping my attention on one thing at a time. In my first year as an artist, all I did was mixed-media collage. I would "creatively glue" all day long. When I wasn't making collages, I was cutting up images and organizing them. I wanted something more, but didn't know what. Then, while searching online, I found the art journal pages of Teesha Moore and Ingrid Dijkers. I was hooked.

Art journaling allowed me the freedom of mixing collages with painting and words. I could test the waters and finally found my artistic voice. Since then I have done art dolls and assemblage, and I finally found the courage to do straight painting, where I come alive. When I have a paintbrush in my hand, I feel different. I am more alive and content. There are no problems in the world, no one exists, and I finally am calm.

When I hit a wall with painting or get a bit bored, I switch to art dolls or assemblages. I still haven't discovered all that I want to do artistically. My mind is churning with all sorts of artistic aspirations. Maybe yours is full of the same creative longings; if only there were more hours in a day! Give yourself permission to do the thing that will make you feel complete. You will be able to live an artful life.

> **GIVE YOURSELF PERMISSION TO DO THE THING THAT WILL MAKE YOU FEEL COMPLETE.**

Suzan Buckner, *Sanity*. 10" × 11" (25.5 × 28 cm). Assemblage on found wood.

Suzan Buckner, *Rust Meets Rhinestones*. 7" × 9" (18 × 23 cm). Funnel assemblage with doll head and mixed media.

I am
not
ready
for you
to
go

you

HEARTFELT COLLAGE

by Brandie Butcher-Isley

Instead of buying new images, I collect old photographs to use as foundations for collage. Whether these pictures evoke my own memories or events in the lives of others, a photograph is the focus of each piece of art I create. Sometimes the idea comes first, and I search for the perfect photograph to express it. Other times a photograph will generate an idea. I often use a photograph with a person in it; the mood and the pose of the person in the photo are pivotal. The person becomes the storyteller as well as the center of the finished work.

MATERIALS

- Assorted paper ephemera, including an old book you don't mind tearing up
- Canvas board
- Matte medium
- Fluid acrylic paints: violet oxide, micaceous iron oxide, titanium white, Payne's gray, sap green, dark blue
- Airbrush medium
- Glazing liquid
- Laser copy of a photograph with an image of a person (must be waterproof ink)*
- Soft graphite pencil
- Water-soluble crayons: light blue and black
- Words or phrases cut from vintage papers
- Colored pencil: black
- White pigment ink pen
- Gloss medium/varnish

If your at-home printer is an ink-jet printer, go to a copy center and make photocopies using a color or black-and-white laser copier.

TOOLS

- Assorted paintbrushes
- Old toothbrush
- Rags
- Sandpaper
- Assorted items to create texture, such as shot glass, corrugated scrapbook paper, sequin waste, craft knife
- Ruler
- Paper punch
- Small scissors

Brandie Butcher-Isley, *Heartfelt Collage*.
5" × 7" (12.5 × 18 cm). Mixed-media collage on canvas panel.

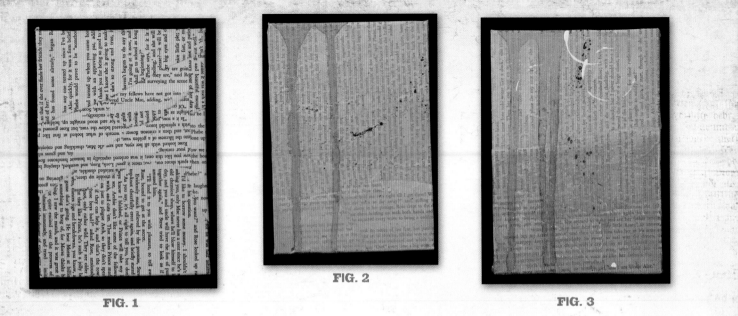

FIG. 1

FIG. 2

FIG. 3

1 Tear several pages out of your old book. Coat the canvas with matte medium, apply a book page, and then brush matte medium on top of the paper. Allow the paper to wrinkle for texture. Continue until the canvas is completely covered. Allow to dry overnight (**Figure 1**).

2 Set up some paper or your old book open next to you. When you have extra paint, use your texture tools to apply it to the book or paper for later use.

3 Mix violet oxide paint with a drop of micaceous iron oxide paint and add airbrush medium to your paint mixture in a two-to-one ratio of paint to medium. Place your canvas in an upright position (a tabletop easel works well for this). Drip the paint mixture down the surface (**Figure 2**).

4 Place iron oxide paint on a toothbrush and spatter the paint across the surface. Allow to dry.

5 Mix white paint with just a drop of Payne's gray to make a sky-blue shade. Create a transparent glaze by adding matte medium in a one-to-one ratio with the paint and put one coat of the mixture on your surface. Allow it to dry for about 30 seconds.

Take a dry rag and lightly wipe off paint. Repeat two more times. Allow to dry completely. Sand the entire piece to bring out your torn paper edges for texture. Mix sap green paint and matte medium in a two-to-one ratio. Paint the surface with this mixture where you would like the ground color to be. Rub the paint off with a rag. Repeat twice (**Figure 3**).

6 Dip a shot glass or other textural object into white paint and stamp on the piece. Spatter white paint with a toothbrush. Allow to dry. Sand.

7 Add more green paint to the horizon line for depth. Add dark blue paint to the horizon and blend in.

8 Mix a blue color a few shades darker than the sky. Paint onto corrugated scrapbook paper, press onto the surface, and pull off for texture. Blend it into the background a little with glazing liquid.

9 Paint the trees (I used undiluted Payne's gray for the trees in the forefront and a lighter tone for the tree in the background). Sand the entire surface lightly (**Figure 4**).

FIG. 4

FIG. 5

10 Place the image of a person on the surface where you want it to be in the finished piece. Trace around it with your graphite pencil. Set it aside to glue on later.

11 Sketch a little house on the horizon. Sketch wings onto your outline of your person (**Figure 5**). Using your ruler, draw flower stems randomly around where the image of the person will stand. Draw a line from the top of the piece for a heart.

12 Paint the house violet oxide. Mix white paint with matte medium in a one-to-one ratio and paint the wings. They should be slightly transparent. Add more detail to the trees; add another layer or two of paint to them and branch them out a bit. Spatter white paint with a toothbrush. Allow to dry.

13 Use your paper punch to punch circles for flowers out of the painted paper you made in step 2. With matte medium, glue a circle to the top of each flower stem. Cut out a heart and a door from your papers. With matte medium, glue the door onto the house and glue your heart on the line you drew in step 11.

14 Stroke a few lines of light blue crayon across the wings. Use glazing liquid to blend the crayon lines. Using black crayon, outline the wings and the house and draw windows on the house. Outline the flowers in the forefront and the heart. Dip a small brush into in glazing liquid and blend your crayon outlines into solid lines. Scratch some of the black off and blend it a little in other areas (I softened this technique around the flowers and the heart). Blend the windows on the house and scratch around them.

15 With matte medium, glue the image of the person where you drew the outline. Outline the image with black crayon. Blend the line as you did in step 14. With the black crayon, scribble around areas for shading. Blend with glazing liquid. Paint or sketch on your person if you like.

16 With matte medium, glue on words and phrases cut from vintage papers. Outline them with the black crayon and blend with glazing liquid. Use the black colored pencil to define the flower stems and the string that the heart hangs from. Add lines with the white pigment pen. Allow the white ink to dry.

17 Coat the whole piece with gloss medium/varnish. Allow to dry. Add another coat.

REINING IN THE STASH

by Alisha Fredrickson
and Glenda Bailey

One of the most exciting things about being a mixed-media artist is the ability to follow your own rules and fashion your own creative process. Nothing is off limits and just about every art medium can cross over and become fodder for a new project. Experimenting is fun!

At TwoCoolTexans, our art studio, we've found that frequently changing the type of projects that we work on helps our creative flow and keeps our attention and interest. We work primarily in collage and assemblage, but also in sewing, needlefelting, encaustic, embroidery, bookmaking, painting, photography, and clay. With so many supplies for all the media we use, keeping it all under control can be overwhelming.

To prevent spending hours just trying to find what we need, we have to be organized. We allot shelves or cabinets for specific supplies such as fabrics, clay, encaustic waxes and tools, wool roving, lace, rubber stamps, stencils, found objects, and substrates such as watercolor paper and canvas. We put away the materials for one project before starting on another in a different medium.

Clockwise from top left:
Glenda Bailey, *Butterflies and Roses.*
6" × 8" (15 × 20.5 cm). Fabric collage.

Glenda Bailey, *Sitting on Her Eggs.*
6" × 8" (15 × 20.5 cm). Collage and assemblage.

Alisha Fredrickson, *The Dance Recital.* 6" × 8"
(15 × 20.5 cm) Collage and assemblage on canvas.

Alisha Fredrickson, *Mom's Rose Cuff.* 2½" × 7½"
(6.5 × 19 cm). Needlepunch and fabric collage.

To begin a new project, we pull out everything that we plan to use and lay everything related to a theme or medium out on our work surface. We keep our tools and supplies close by as we work. We each have specific stations or work areas—a computer and printing area, a sewing area, and a space for painting and stamping.

We keep most of our supplies in tubs, clear plastic bins, and on shelves. Even our rubber stamps are on narrow shelves attached inside the closet or on a wall so that each stamp can be seen at a glance. We keep unmounted stamps in small plastic drawers, separated by theme. Wool, felt, laces, and other fabrics are separated according to type and color in large clear plastic bins with snap-on lids. Magazines, books, and tools are on open shelves.

For us, out of sight, is definitely out of mind. We display as much as possible so that it can easily be seen when a closet door or cabinet is opened. Large pieces of paper, such as watercolor papers, are kept tightly rolled up and stored in a very large plastic trash can. We store decorative papers in rolling carts with dividers. Small collage papers are sorted by color in shoe boxes. Beads and charms are in well-labeled small plastic storage boxes.

Even with all this planning, sometimes piles of supplies accumulate. We each need a different amount of neatness to do our best work. Finding just the right amount of creative chaos to keep the wheels turning and the creativity marching on is an important step in the creative process.

VINTAGE-LOOK PHOTO COLLAGE

Creating a collage of images is easy and fast if you use a substrate with a background already prepared; this also limits the number of new supplies you'll need. I use Derivan Liquid Pencil to give new photos and the entire collage a vintage feel. Liquid Pencil looks like gray heavy-body acrylic paint with graphite sheen. When dry, the permanent version can be burnished like traditional pencil. The re-wettable version can be lifted with an eraser and reworked like watercolor.

MATERIALS

- Substrate of your choosing with prepared background (see page 21)
- Color or black-and-white copy of a photo
- Derivan Liquid Pencil (rewettable) in the tint of your choice
- White charcoal pencil
- Workable spray fixative
- Charcoal
- White pen
- Soft matte gel medium
- Additional elements such as text, paper scraps, or more collage images
- Water-soluble crayons
- Graphite pencil
- White paint
- Acrylic sealant

TOOLS

- Blue painter's tape
- Paintbrushes
- Eraser
- Dip pen (such as those used for pen and ink drawing)
- Blending stump
- Awl or other sharp tool
- Rags or paper towels

Pam Carriker, *Vintage-Look Photo Collage*. 8" × 15¾" (20.5 × 40 cm). Mixed-media collage on canvas.

FIG. 1

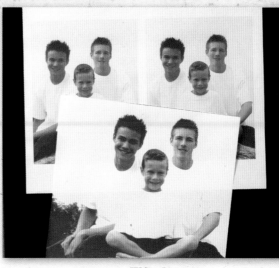

FIG. 2

1 Choose a substrate with a prepared background (**Figure 1**).

2 Choose a photo and make a copy at a size that fits the substrate (**Figure 2**).

3 Use blue painter's tape to fix the photocopy to your work surface; the tape will keep the photocopy flat as you work. Place a small amount of Liquid Pencil on your palette, add water, and mix with a small brush to a watercolor consistency. Begin painting on your photocopy with a light layer of Liquid Pencil in the areas that are shadowed in your photo. Continue building layers of Liquid Pencil to create deeper shadows where needed. Use the photo as your guide to show you where the darks and lights should be. Let dry (**Figure 3**).

4 Use an eraser to erase areas of Liquid Pencil to establish the highlights. Use the white charcoal pencil to further enhance highlights (**Figure 4**).

5 Using your dip pen, pick up a few drops of the diluted Liquid Pencil. Sketch in detail areas on your image and embellish as desired.

6 Spray with a workable fixative to set the Liquid Pencil. Set aside.

7 Draw a horizon line on your substrate with charcoal and blend with a blending stump. Make a wash of one-third Liquid Pencil and two-thirds water and apply the wash to the bottom of the horizon line. Let dry (**Figure 5**).

8 Add some journaling with a white pen.

9 Use a soft gel medium to adhere the altered photo to the substrate, painting a layer of medium over the front of the image as well.

10 Add additional text and elements in the same way as desired.

FIG. 3

FIG. 4

11 Determine the direction of your light source and shade the opposite areas around the images using any color of water-soluble crayon. Using a wet paintbrush, activate the crayon and manipulate it as desired.

12 Further enhance the shaded areas with a wash of Liquid Pencil.

13 Use a graphite pencil to trace around some of the images. Erase some areas of the ground to uncover hidden text.

14 Use the awl to scratch additional journaling into the background and go over it with a wash of Liquid Pencil. Before the wash dries, wipe off excess wash with a rag or paper towel, leaving the Liquid Pencil in the scratch marks.

15 Use water-soluble crayon and activate with a wet brush to add color where desired. Add some drips of white paint.

16 Spray the finished piece with an acrylic sealant using several light coats.

FIG. 5

SEVEN-DAY JOURNAL
DAY 2: IMAGE TRANSFER

Transferring images and adding collage elements are two of my favorite ways to embellish art journal pages. A combination of collage and image transfers gives depth to your work. There are several different ways to transfer an image to a journal page. Instructions for my favorite transfer techniques follow, but try different methods to find your own favorite.

MY FAVORITE TRANSFER TECHNIQUE

Don't worry if your transfers are imperfect; I love the look of partially transferred images in my journal. It gives character to the pages and adds to the decaying, vintage feel. I learned this transfer method from artist Glenda Bailey.

MATERIALS
- Printable images or text
- Transparency blanks
- Gel hand sanitizer
- Ten-minute journal (page 24) with prepared backgrounds

TOOLS
- Inkjet printer
- Scissors
- Sponge brush
- Bone folder or spoon for burnishing

1 Print the images or text onto a transparency blank using an inkjet printer.

2 Trim around the image, leaving a ¼" (6 mm) border.

3 Using a sponge brush, apply gel hand sanitizer to the area of the image that you wish to transfer.

4 Place the image, ink side down, onto the journal page, and gently pat to ensure good contact.

5 Burnish with a bone folder or spoon until the image has transferred. If you lift up the transparency and it hasn't completely transferred, add a bit more hand sanitizer and burnish again.

Pam Carriker, *Seven-Day Journal*. 8" × 8" (20.5 × 20.5 cm) closed. Handmade journal with mixed-media pages.

EASY COLLAGE METHOD

Collage adds personality to your journal pages. Choose images that will help tell the story of you. Digital collage sheets are readily available and a great source of inspiration, but introduce a variety of images for individuality.

MATERIALS
- Paper and images to collage, such as vintage papers and digital collage sheets
- Ten-Minute Journal (page 24) with prepared backgrounds
- Soft gel medium

TOOLS
- Scissors or craft knife
- Sponge brush

1 Tear or cut out collage elements that you want to use.

2 Try out different placements on the page until you're satisfied.

3 Using the sponge brush, apply soft gel medium to the back of the collage element and then to the area on a journal page where it will be placed.

4 Place the image on the journal page.

5 Burnish the image with your fingers to ensure good contact and to work out any air bubbles.

6 Add more soft gel medium to the image.

7 Keep working in this way until all of your collage elements are in place.

CHAPTER 3

CREATING CYBER-SPACE AND SETTING LIMITS

THE HONEY-MAKER.   159

Pleasant words are a honeycomb,
sweet to the soul and healing to the bones.

PROVERBS 16 VERSE 24

planning and limit-setting, you can integrate all that technology has to offer into your artful life and watch your creativity grow before your very eyes.

> ### SAYING NO IS OKAY, AND YOU NEED TO GIVE YOURSELF PERMISSION TO KEEP YOUR APPOINTMENT WITH YOUR MUSE.

Some days it can seem like everyone wants a piece of you until there's little or nothing left of the "artist formerly known as (your name here)." Boundaries around your creative time are essential. When others make demands on your time for art, you need to protect that time and let go of any guilt. Saying no is okay, and you need to give yourself permission to keep your appointment with your muse. Computers can steal your time, too. Anyone who's ever fallen down the rabbit hole in the Land of Blogs knows this well. The online world can also save you time, however, with online workshops, shopping for hard-to-find supplies, selling artwork, and building a platform for your budding art career. With some careful

Whether expanding your online presence or adding a new medium such as the PaperClay that Sue Pelletier uses in this chapter's *Artist Spotlight* project, adding layers of texture to your art life enriches both the process and the product! This chapter also includes a *Speed of Life* Project to achieve a papier-mâché look with things you already have around the house. As you continue on in the *Seven-Day Journal* project, adding layers becomes child's play with options for creating interesting and textural surfaces in your journal pages.

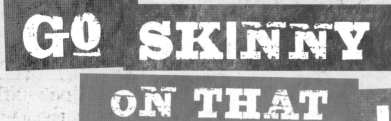

GO SKINNY ON THAT LATTE

Ordering my daily brew has become a habit. Raised near Seattle, where espresso is brewed on every street corner, it's fun to hear people rattle off their personal perfect cup of joe; they know what they want. "I'll have a short skinny mocha to go, hold the foam." The lingo sounds complicated, but it's easy to understand by breaking it down. Apply the language of the coffee barista (with a little twist) to your creative life, and you, too, can set limits and order up exactly what you need and want.

To go. This is a great state of mind to be in when you get the urge to create. I'll often grab a portable basket from my studio and toss in supplies for a project. I carry it around the house and work on my art in between other daily activities. Most days I end up in bed with my basket, still working!

Skinny. Shorthand for skim milk in coffee language, this is about setting calorie limits for yourself; the same tactic is necessary to find extra creative time. I try to "skinny up" whenever possible. Use your phone to instantly alert you to e-mail so you don't feel overwhelmed later by a full mailbox. Or keep your computer near your art area to do quick checks of e-mail, blogs, or shops as you wait for paint layers to dry.

Hold the foam. I set a time limit for forums and social media sites—say, as long as it takes to drink a cup of coffee. If I have to get up to re-heat it, I've been there too long!

The quad. At the coffee shop, if I'm really dragging, I go for the quad, four delicious I-can-feel-my-hair-move shots of espresso. I use this approach in my work as well to get a lot done in a short amount of time. I'll set up multiple projects on my work space, moving back and forth between them. When working in series or even just a similar color palette, this helps save time and supplies.

Pam Carriker, *Love a Latté*. 8" × 8" (20.5 × 20.5 cm). Mixed-media collage with acrylic paint.

GOOD THINGS COME IN SMALL PACKAGES

Thinking big is great, but thinking small can have big benefits, too. Being creative every day does not necessarily mean completing a piece of work. The goal is to be creative in some way, every day. View every step in the process as an accomplishment. By setting limits on the size of your work, you can play with speed and scale and produce many finished pieces.

> **VIEW EVERY STEP IN THE PROCESS AS AN ACCOMPLISHMENT.**

Artist trading cards (ATCs) are small pieces of original artwork that measure 2½" × 3½" (6.5 × 9 cm). If I'm really bent on completing a piece of art, but lack the time for a large project, ATCs can really fit my needs. As the name implies, artists often trade ATCs. You can also make them in series; grouped together, matted, and framed, they can add up to pieces of substance.

Create a background on a large piece of paper or other substrate and then cut it into ATC-size pieces ready for artful additions such as journaling, collage, transfers, even a little drawing or painting. When working small, you can work on several pieces at once, and when you're done pat yourself on the back for creating multiple works of art in one day!

These miniature works of art can come in very handy for art exchanges, small gifts, or even as affordable works to sell. There are books available that focus on techniques for creating ATCs, but more than anything they should be a reflection of your work, so try to scale down things you already do in large work.

> **WORK ON SEVERAL PIECES AT ONCE, AND WHEN YOU'RE DONE PAT YOURSELF ON THE BACK.**

THE JOY OF BLOGGING

by Dawn Edmonson

If you don't yet have a blog, jump on the bandwagon and give it a try. A blog can generate interest in a business and help establish wonderful relationships with your customers as you gather comments and post weekly photos of new shop arrivals.

I discovered the world of blogging as a marketing tool for my antiques store, and I was hooked! My store blog led to a personal blog to share found treasures, thoughts on daily life, and my creations. Posting work on my blog opened the door to all kinds of possibilities, from selling work to getting it published. Most amazing, I receive support and encouragement from readers and friends. Blogging made it possible for me to pursue art full time.

Blogging almost daily enables me to enjoy interaction with friends and to pay the goodness forward by introducing new bloggers to my readers and sharing techniques. Having a blog gives me accountability to make time to create, even if it's for just a little while, and that's important in the midst of busy lives. It nurtures the soul. Here are some of my keys to successful blogging:.

Dawn Edmonson, *Love Much.* 11" × 14" (28 × 35.5 cm). Collage with paper frame, fabric heart, sheet music, and key.

- Blog often to establish a faithful following. Readers will come when they know there's always something new to see.
- Use your blog to promote others. Foster an inspiring, encouraging atmosphere.
- Be yourself! Establish a homey feel that invites readers in.
- Use your blog to motivate yourself! Posting frequently pushes you to create frequently.

IMPROVE YOUR BLOG WITH DRIVE-BY POSTING

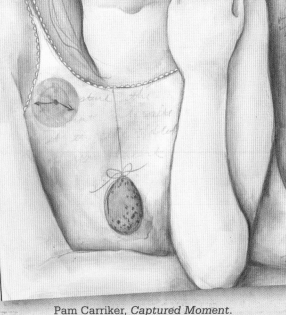

Pam Carriker, *Captured Moment*.
9" × 12" (23 × 30.5 cm). Acrylic paint and collage on watercolor paper.

I've never even met most of the friends on my social networking site! With blogs to visit and visitors coming to our own blogs, we connect through the common bond of art. By simply commenting on someone's blog, I might find myself visiting several more sites, full of inspiration and eye candy. Before I know it, a major amount of time has passed by—time that might have been better spent creating some of my own art.

Don't stop blog-hopping completely, but do set limits on this activity. I like to write, and to read, what I call *drive-by postings*: pictures with a little bit of text, rather than tombs of writing that take forever to wade through. Why not blog this way? Think of it as the movie trailer, not the whole film. Leave them wanting more! Posting is a breeze, and I've also noticed that more people tend to comment on a shorter post, or they'll comment on more than one post. You should be able to see most of your post without even having to scroll down. I find that frequent short posts are more effective on my blog than longer, less frequent ones.

I like to set aside a certain time of day to spend blogging. I love to sit in the morning with my second cup of coffee, checking out the latest on my friends' blogs and posting something to mine. I feel connected to the whole art community. Try it!

EMBRACE ONLINE POSSIBILITIES

by Gail Schmidt

I've always had a shopkeeper gene residing in me. I used to dream of having a beautiful little store and living in an apartment above. After years of working in office environments, I discovered I had a talent for painting. I embarked on a new journey, eventually owning my quaint, adorable shop. I set up a studio area in the store where I could paint and teach decorative painting classes. My dream had finally come true, but then my husband and I decided to move to the mountains of Tennessee.

When we were settled in our new home, a seventy-five-year-old farm cottage, I once again opened a shop/studio, adding custom murals and faux finishes to the business. But things were different. I woke up one day to the reality that it wasn't going to happen here in this place, and

Gail Schmidt, *Altered Child's Board Book*. 8" × 11" (20.5 × 28 cm) closed. Mixed-media journal.

I was beginning to feel burned out; it was time to shut everything down. The idea of picking up a paintbrush made me feel dreadful, and I began to fear I would never be creative again.

Then one day I was online looking for something, and like Alice, I fell into a marvelous, magical world—the world of mixed media, collage, and altered art. I fell in love with this new world. I became more involved online and began to join groups, in turn meeting other wonderfully warm and amazing artists. I took a deep breath and decided to open an online store where I could sell both art and art supplies. I opened Shabby Cottage Studio in October 2007.

Follow my example and don't give up if changes in your life leave you wondering what your next artistic step will be. Stay open to the possibilities in your new reality, and your path will open up. And it might just be selling your work online!

Gail Schmidt, *Treasures Box*. 7½" × 9" (19 × 23 cm). Fabric collage.

PAPIER-MÂCHÉ DRESSES COLLAGE

by Sue Pelletier

Even though we all live in a modern, super-connected present, I like to stay grounded by expressing my remembrances of the past. Often my work is inspired by a moment or a memory that has stayed with me for years, such as a book called *A Hundred Dresses* by Eleanor Estes. Poking through an antique store one day, I came across a single paper-doll dress, reminding me of the story. It inspired me to create my own series of a hundred dresses with the simplicity of childhood paper-doll drawings.

MATERIALS

- Brown Kraft paper
- Drop cloth, unprimed canvas, or heavy muslin, 10" × 10" (25.5 × 25.5 cm)
- Gauze strips
- Plaster mix, such as Paris Craft
- Instant papier-mâché, such as Celluclay
- Heavy matte gel medium
- White tissue paper
- Pattern tissue from old dress patterns
- Colored tissue paper
- Small pieces of muslin with hand or machine stitching
- Water-based oil pastels
- Acrylic paints in your choice of colors
- Black graphite pencil
- Black wax marking pencil
- Wide-edge canvas, 12" × 12" (30.5 × 30.5 cm)
- Collage materials such as papers, fabric or quilt scraps, flash cards, words, and drawings
- Metal embellishments such as nails, charms, or brads, and nails to attach them
- Wire to make coat hanger and wire staple
- Small clothespins

TOOLS

- Paintbrushes
- Hammer

Sue Pelletier, *Papier-Mâché Dresses Collage.* 12" × 12" (30.5 × 30.5 cm). PaperClay and papier-mâché on canvas.

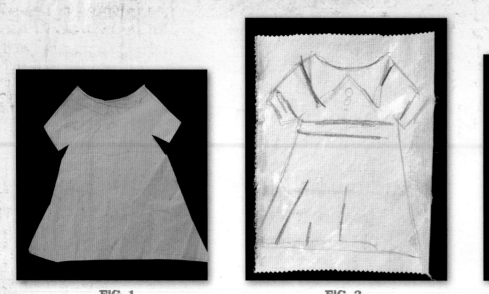

FIG. 1   FIG. 2   FIG. 3

1 Loosely sketch a dress on brown Kraft paper to use as a pattern. It should be smaller than your wide-edge canvas **(Figure 1)**.

2 Using the brown paper pattern, draw the dress form onto a piece of drop cloth, unprimed canvas, or heavy muslin **(Figure 2)**.

3 On the drop cloth, canvas, or muslin, begin to build up the dress form using gauze strips and plaster. Wet the plaster strips and drape them on the canvas, staying within your sketch lines. Use the plaster to create folds to mimic the folds in clothing. Let the plaster dry overnight **(Figure 3)**.

4 Using instant papier-mâché mixed with water, begin adding detail to the dress, adding more folds as well as collar and sleeve details. Allow to dry for 48 hours.

5 Using gel medium, apply white tissue paper over the entire dress form and let dry **(Figure 4)**.

6 Using gel medium diluted with water, begin collaging onto the dress with tissue from old dress patterns, colored tissue paper, and bits of muslin with some stitching added. Allow to dry.

7 Add color to the dress with water-based oil pastels, acrylic paints, black graphite pencil, and black wax marking pencil **(Figure 5)**.

8 Create a background on your canvas. Using gel medium, attach paper, quilt scraps, flash cards, words, and drawings, or whatever you like. Allow everything to dry **(Figure 6)**.

9 Build up layers with color. I draw on both the canvas background and the dresses with water-based oil pastels, applied dry or with a wet paintbrush. Add detail and shading to the dress. While pastel areas are wet, use a graphite pencil to scribble and scrape the pastel away. Use the pencil to outline polka dots or details for a border. Use the black wax marking pencil to outline the dress,

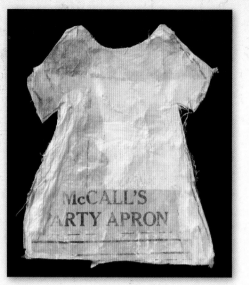

FIG. 4

FIG. 5

FIG. 6

adding lines to the background. Dry-brush layers of paint onto the background and the dress **(Figure 7)**.

10 Lay the dress on the canvas and observe how things are beginning to work together and how colors and textures begin to blend and complement each other. Add metal embellishments to the piece, such as nails, charms, or brads, nailing them directly into the wood edge of the canvas.

11 Determine where you want to place the dress on the canvas. Twist and shape the wire to make a coat hanger. Attach the dress with small clothespins to the hanger; add gel medium if needed to help it adhere. Use a wire staple poked through the canvas with a bit of gel medium to attach the hanger to the canvas.

FIG. 7

BE AN A+ STUDENT IN ONLINE WORKSHOPS

by Paulette Insall

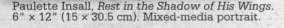

Paulette Insall, *Rest in the Shadow of His Wings.* 6" × 12" (15 × 30.5 cm). Mixed-media portrait.

Online classes offer the comfort and convenience of working in your own home at your own pace, with the added benefits of downloadable video demonstrations, printable documents, class blogs, social network class sites, discussion forums, and live chats. Online classes also give you continued access to a community of other artists. In online classes I've taken and taught, I've seen connections and friendships formed between fellow students that lasted long after the class was over. They are able to share their art and themselves in a way that is nearly impossible to do during a traditional class.

As a teacher, online classes have opened up a new world to me. Traveling to teach in person isn't something I can easily do. By offering classes online, I'm able to share my knowledge with so many more people. I've had people in my classes from all over the world. In an online class environment, students progress at their own pace and really learn the techniques rather than just get a brief exposure in a one-day class. When my students share their progress through posting pictures online, I get to witness their growth and see the end result of their time spent learning the techniques.

When you're ready to teach, online workshops are a great way to go. As a student, you can gain so much from online workshops with a little planning. Try these tips to be a successful student:

- Choose a class from an artist whose work you are drawn to. Read the class description, check out the supply list, ask other attendees for feedback, and don't hesitate to ask questions.
- Go into the class with an open mind, intending to learn the techniques and apply them. Classes aren't usually a paint-by-number deal; they're for gaining new tools to implement in your own creative way.
- Every teacher has an individual style. If you find a teacher's style isn't right for you, find a different teacher for your next experience.
- Be courteous. If you have a problem, direct it to the teacher first. Everyone comes to class with the intent to learn and have fun, so it's important not to ruin that for others.
- Sharing is a big part of the community that an online class creates. Seeing what everyone creates with the lessons given is inspiring. But the teacher works hard to prepare a class, so don't share your lessons with friends who haven't paid for the class.

SCHOOL DAZE!

When you're ready to start exploring online classes for mixed-media art, try these virtual classrooms.

All Norah's Art
allnorahsart.ning.com

Craft Edu
community.craftedu.com

Creative Workshops
creativeworkshops.ning.com

Les Petite Academy
suziblu.ning.com

Violette's Creative Juice
freakflag.ca/workshops

Visual Poetry
web.me.com/hgtuttle3rd/VPPublic/Workshops.html

Paulette Insall, *Without Ceasing*.
8" × 8" (20.5 × 20.5 cm). Mixed-media portrait.

IF YOU FIND A TEACHER'S STYLE ISN'T RIGHT FOR YOU, FIND A DIFFERENT TEACHER FOR YOUR NEXT EXPERIENCE.

TOILETTE

PAPIER-MÂCHÉ

This is a fast, easy, inexpensive way to get the look of papier-mâché and paper clay with no mess. (I thought the fancy French "toilette" was classier than "toilet paper.") The end result can be incorporated onto canvas, cards, or art journal pages, giving texture and dimension to your work. I made my own foam stamps for this project, but you can use stamps that you already have and begin with step 4.

MATERIALS

- Foam or rubber stamps with bold designs, or 1 sheet of thin adhesive-backed craft foam and 1 sheet of ½" (1.3 cm) craft foam to make your own stamps
- Roll of toilet paper
- Soft gel medium or white school glue
- Canvas with prepared background (see page 21)
- Wire
- 2 brads or small nails
- Golden brand Tar Gel
- Acrylic paints
- Charcoal pencil
- Permanent marker

TOOLS

- If making own stamps, scrap paper, graphite pencil, scissors, X-acto knife
- Towel
- Spray water bottle
- Wire cutters
- Hammer
- Paintbrushes
- Blending stump

Pam Carriker. *Toilette Papier-Mâché.*
8" × 16" (20.5 × 40.5 cm). Toilet paper and acrylic paint collage.

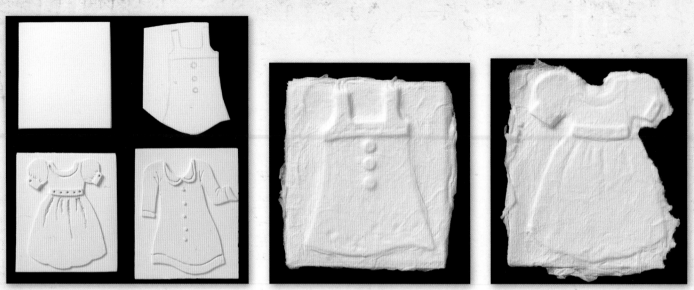

FIG. 1 FIG. 2 FIG. 3

1 Draw a simple dress design onto scrap paper using a graphite pencil (**Figure 1**).

2 Turn the paper over onto the thin adhesive-backed foam sheet and rub with your fingers to easily transfer the design. Cut out the design and adhere it by peeling off the backing and positioning the sticky side of the foam to the ½" (1.3 cm) craft foam. Cut away excess.

3 Add additional details by carving into the foam and adding raised details cut from the excess adhesive-backed foam sheet. You can transfer an additional copy of your design and cut details from that to add to the stamp. You don't need a lot of detail; a bold design works best.

4 Lay your stamp on a towel face up.

5 Separate squares of toilet paper; you'll need about 10 to 15. If it's two-ply tissue, separate the plies.

6 Fill the water bottle with about 1 cup (236 ml) of warm water and 2 tablespoons (30 ml) of soft gel medium or glue. Shake until thoroughly mixed.

7 Lay a piece of toilet paper onto the stamp and spritz with the water mixture. It'll become almost transparent and form to the shape of the stamp's design. Repeat this with about four more pieces of toilet paper, laying them randomly to produce an uneven edge. Gently press around the design to remove air bubbles.

8 Continue adding toilet paper, spritzing, and patting until you have an opaque, fairly thick buildup. Stop before you lose design details (**Figure 2**).

9 Let dry. You can place it in front of a fan to speed the drying process, checking periodically for the development of air bubbles and patting them out if they occur.

FIG. 4

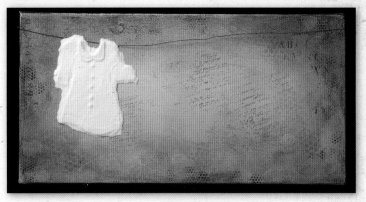

FIG. 5

10 When the faux papier-mâché is completely dry, gently lift it off the stamp.

11 Carefully tear around the design if necessary, leaving a little edge to adhere to the canvas (**Figures 3 and 4**).

12 Add a clothesline to the canvas by attaching a thin wire to two brads nailed to either end.

13 Apply a thick coat of soft gel medium to the back of the dresses and place onto the prepared background, slightly above the wire clothesline. Gently pat to ensure good contact and apply a thin coat of soft gel medium to the top. Be careful not to oversaturate the paper with water or you'll lose your image details. Let dry thoroughly (**Figure 5**).

14 Add a scroll detail and a numeral 3 to the canvas with a small paintbrush and some Tar Gel. Let this dry thoroughly (**Figure 6**).

FIG. 6

15 Add paint to the background and the dresses to tie them together. The Tar Gel will create a resist effect, allowing the underlying layers to show through the paint.

16 Shade around the dresses with a charcoal pencil and blend it into the background with a blending stump.

17 Add text or journaling with a permanent marker if desired.

SEVEN-DAY JOURNAL
DAY 3: ADDING TEXTURE

Adding textural elements to journal pages is the next step in our journal project. In the spirit of setting limits, it's possible to add texture and keep your book's slim profile. I use raised texture on a couple of pages, but not every page, so my journal still closes comfortably. Adding textural elements helps me audition materials and methods for my artwork. I document the process and my findings right on the journal page.

MATERIALS

- Ten-Minute Journal with prepared backgrounds (page 24)
- Light molding paste
- Fluid acrylic paint
- Baby wipes (those you've already used to wipe paint are fine)
- Soft gel medium
- Leftover bits of faux papier-mâché made with toilet paper (page 63)

TOOLS

- Stencils
- Palette knife or old credit card
- Sponge brush
- Paintbrushes

MOLDING PASTE RELIEF

1 Lay a stencil on one of your pages.

2 Using your palette knife or an old credit card, scoop a bit of light molding paste from the container and scrape it across the stencil.

3 Lift the stencil straight up from the page and position it on another part of the page, repeating the process as many times as you like to get hints of texture.

4 Let the light molding paste dry completely.

5 Mix fluid acrylic paint and water in a one-to-two ratio and use this mixture to paint a light wash with the sponge brush onto the molding paste texture. Let dry.

Pam Carriker, *Seven-Day Journal.*
8" × 8" (20.5 × 20.5 cm) closed. Handmade journal with mixed-media pages.

BABY WIPE TEXTURE

1 Tear a used baby wipe into strips to give it a softly feathered edge.

2 Adhere the strips to parts of your pages with soft gel medium.

3 Allow bits of the baby wipe to hang over the edge of the page for a soft, uneven, interesting look.

4 When the soft gel medium has dried, add paint if desired.

FAUX PAPIER-MÂCHÉ

This method adds leftover bits of faux papier-mâché (from the project on page 63) to the journal page. Don't oversaturate the shape with medium. Add this type of texture to only a few pages, or your journal will be hard to close.

1 Apply a thick layer of soft gel medium to the back of the faux papier-mâché shape.

2 Position the shape on the journal page and gently pat to ensure good contact. Let dry.

3 Add more soft gel medium to the front of the faux papier-mâché shape; let dry.

4 Add paint to the faux papier-mâché if desired.

CREATING CYBER-SPACE AND SETTING LIMITS

CHAPTER 4

ART THERAPY

Art means different things to different people, but most agree it can be therapeutic. So take your medicine by making art! If you have days when this just doesn't seem possible, if work, family, and other commitments overwhelm you, take a step back and reevaluate your situation. With creative planning, you can clear a path to more productive, creative time. Leading a creative life means finding peace within you. Use art to help you deal with life's stresses. Walk the tightrope between your daily life and your creative life with an umbrella in your hand and a safety net below—but walk it! There is healing power in taking action.

LEADING A CREATIVE LIFE MEANS FINDING PEACE WITHIN YOU.

This chapter brings you essays and projects designed to help you make the most of the therapeutic power of art. An encaustic project from Glenda Bailey uses an age-old medium to produce a serene piece of artwork. If you don't have time to heat things up, try the *Speed of Life* version, using my Busy Beeswax formula, to get the warm, soft look of wax quickly and easily. Then add another layer to the pages of your art journal using resist techniques in the ongoing *Seven-Day Journal* project!

TIME IS WHAT WE WANT MOST, BUT . . . WHAT WE USE WORST.
–WILLIAM PENN

Art Credits: page 143

ART ATTACK

Ever have one of *those* days, when your muse is dancing around on your shoulder, begging to be let loose, but your brain is telling you all of the things you ought to be doing instead of creating? The tug-of-war between being practical and missing a creative moment happens to most of us at one time or another, and though it's easy to say that you don't want to miss your chance for creative inspiration, reality sometimes wins out.

If you don't have time for open-ended creativity when you're in the mood, don't let it stress you out. Think about the things you can do, such as sketch for a few minutes to capture your inspiration. Maybe you have time to clear a space on your worktable and set out tools and materials. Or, best of all, decide to set aside some of the tasks on your to-do list for a later time, in favor of art.

Perhaps you can only mentally prepare for the moment you'll be able to pick up that paintbrush. Let that moment unfold in your mind. Close your eyes, visualizing what you want to do. What media will you work in? What colors will be on your palette? Imagine being in your art space with your favorite music playing and no interruptions. Visualize the finished work.

Let your mind return to these mental pictures often until you're able to put them onto canvas. You may find that the end result is not exactly as you pictured, but even better, because you nurtured your inspiration and allowed it to develop before it was executed.

> EVEN IF IT'S NOT POSSIBLE TO ACT ON EACH MOMENT OF INSPIRATION IMMEDIATELY, IT IS POSSIBLE TO LIVE IN THE MOMENT AND ENJOY YOUR CREATIVE SOUL.

So let your muse dance when she wants to dance. Embrace the creativity that lives within you.

Let art help you live your life to the fullest. It's good for the mind and the heart and allows you to share more of yourself with those whose lives you touch.

Pam Carriker, *An Attack of the Heart.*
8" × 8" (20.5 × 20.5 cm). Collage with acrylic paint.

BLOCKED?
READ A BLOG!

by Laurie Blau-Marshall

A few years ago, I experienced the longest bout of artistic block that I have ever had. I'd been making jewelry for about fifteen years, selling in boutiques, galleries, and sometimes out of my purse in impromptu trunk shows. It was a great supplementary income for me, and I often flirted with the idea of making it my only income. After my daughter was born, though, my creativity trickled down to nothing. My supplies were gathering dust. Then I discovered blogs. Beautiful, lyrical, sweet, friendly blogs! What a world! What amazing people! Blogs inspired me to become an artist again and still inspire me every day.

My husband and I moved to the suburbs about two weeks before our baby was born. I loved being with my baby and felt lucky to be able to stay home with her, but I sometimes felt stuck. As my baby grew, she was eventually diagnosed with autism spectrum disorder. I felt monumentally sorry for myself! I also talked myself into a gargantuan case of artist's block.

One day I came across a magazine article that mentioned artist trading cards. Intrigued, I did an Internet search, and what a wonderful world I discovered. Altered art! Mixed media! Collage! It was love at first sight. I found message boards and social networking groups, where I noticed that a lot of people were mentioning that they had started "blogs." I clicked on someone's link, and you know what happened next. That link led to another link, which led to another link, which led to another link … suddenly it was two hours later and I was immersed in a whole new world. Reading those blogs reawakened the artist in me.

These days, when the therapy, tests, and assessments related to my daughter's autism get me down, or when daily life is just too much, I head to the computer to read a few blog posts. Art bloggers are the most generous people in the world. They share their ideas, their techniques, their flea market finds, their trials and tribulations. Whenever I'm feeling blocked, there's always somebody, somewhere, to commiserate with, and someone to inspire me out of it.

> ART BLOGGERS ARE THE MOST GENEROUS PEOPLE IN THE WORLD.

So whenever you're feeling isolated or uninspired, turn to the blog world, with its vast treasures of mixed-media art right at your fingertips. Make friends online with like-minded artists. It just might be the community you're looking for.

Laurie Blau-Marshall, *Watch Me Bloom*.
11" × 14" (28 × 35.5 cm). Vintage dictionary pages, acrylic paint, and ink on canvas.

ENCAUSTIC ENCOUNTER COLLAGE

by Glenda Bailey

I have come to love encaustic, the centuries-old technique of painting layers of beeswax and damar resin. Each layer must be heat-fused to the layer below it. This technique is very forgiving; you can easily fix mistakes by heating the element that you wish to remove and just pulling it off. You can add embellishments of all kinds by just embedding them into the piece with more wax. I find this technique very therapeutic and relaxing, and the ethereal beauty of the finished piece is healing to look at.

MATERIALS

- Cradled hardboard canvas or other rigid absorbent substrate, 6" × 6" × ¾" (15 × 15 × 2 cm)
- Encaustic gesso
- Encaustic medium, 104 ml block
- Vintage ledger paper, 4" × 6" (10 × 15 cm)
- Vintage children's book page
- Tea-dyed or vintage lace, 6" × 3" (15 × 7.5 cm)
- Strip of cardboard, 6" × 1½" (15 × 3.8 cm)
- Twine, 6" (15 cm)
- Metal embellishment such as found metal object or charm
- Small vintage-style image of a child to fit in the metal embellishment (optional)
- Black encaustic paint

TOOLS

- Natural-bristle brushes
- Electric skillet with temperature gauge, or small skillet and griddle or hot plate
- Heat gun
- Scissors
- Tin can, such as a sardine can, for mixing paint and wax
- Popsicle stick
- Old credit card (optional)

Glenda Bailey, *A Token of Remembrance*.
6" × 6" (15 × 15 cm). Encaustic and mixed media on wood.

ESSENTIAL ENCAUSTIC TIPS!

• Encaustic painting involves the use of wax heated to higher than 200°F (93°C). It is extremely important to follow all safety precautions. Work in a well-ventilated area. Keep children and pets away from hot wax. Do not leave heating elements unattended. Wear gloves and a mask.

• No acrylic mediums or paints should be used anywhere in the piece with one exception: collages can be made by using acrylic glue on the underside of paper as long as it doesn't make contact with the wax.

• You can make your own encaustic paint by combining regular artist oil paints with encaustic medium (a combination of beeswax and damar resin).

• Substrates must be porous and rigid for the wax to bond properly. Cracking will eventually occur if encaustics are mounted on a nonrigid surface, or if acrylic paints or gels are used in between the layers.

• Keep your finished artwork out of direct sunlight and don't keep your pieces in the trunk of your car.

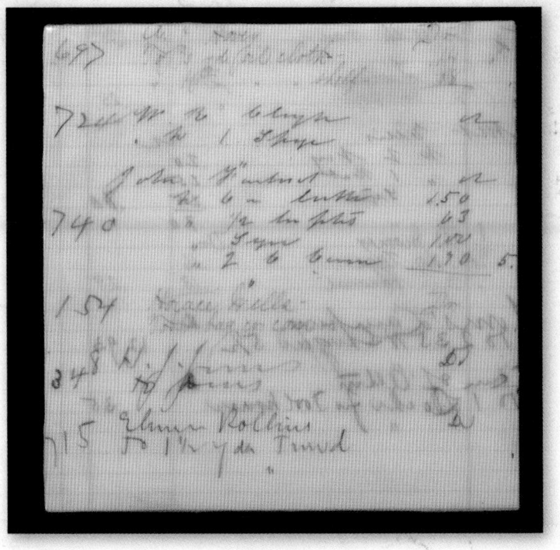

FIG. 1

1 Paint your canvas or substrate with two coats of gesso specifically made for encaustics. Allow to dry.

2 Melt the encaustic medium in the electric skillet or in a small skillet on the griddle or hot plate. The medium melts at about 220°F (104°C). Warm the board with a heat gun and then apply the encaustic medium with a natural-bristle brush. Fuse the medium by heating it with a heat gun until the wax has a slight shine. Apply one more layer of encaustic medium.

3 Cut a large piece of vintage ledger paper to fit the front of the canvas. Heat the wax on the canvas and gently push the paper into the warm wax. Brush on another layer of encaustic medium. Don't worry if the medium drips over the edge a bit or if the wax looks cloudy; as it cools it will become transparent **(Figure 1)**.

4 Take a page from a vintage children's book (or use other paper) and tear to about two-thirds the size of the canvas. Gently heat the medium on the board

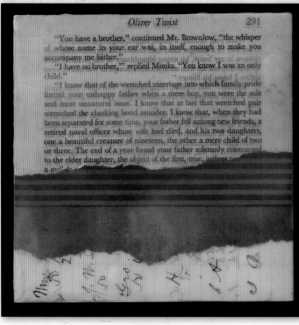

FIG. 2

FIG. 3

with the heat gun and lay the paper down. Apply another coat of wax and fuse with the heat gun to the layer below. Do this with any additional papers desired until the background is complete **(Figure 2)**.

5 Cut a strip of tea-dyed or vintage lace and apply it just as you did the paper by warming the medium, laying the lace in it, applying another coat of medium to the top of the lace, and then heating to fuse **(Figure 3)**.

6 Add a little encaustic medium to the center of the piece and push the piece of cardboard into it. Coat the cardboard with wax. Add the twine and metal embellishment with vintage image inserted, if desired, in the same way, coating each with wax.

7 To complete the piece, put one part black encaustic paint and three parts encaustic medium in the tin can and set it on the griddle at 220°F (104°C). Mix with a Popsicle stick until blended. Using a natural-bristle brush, paint the sides of the cradled

hardboard with the mixture. I like to leave the sides a bit bumpy for additional texture. If you want a smoother look you can gently heat the wax and keep moving it until it's smooth or you can scrape some of the wax off with a tool such as an old credit card.

8 Fuse the sides carefully so as not to disturb the top of the canvas. Add a few drips of wax to the top for visual interest, if desired.

DEADLINE DILEMMA: WHAT GIVES?

by Nancy Lefko

There is joy in sharing artwork and the creative process through workshops, art blogs, online tutorials, and writing articles for magazines and books. When I was asked to write my first article I was thrilled! But the euphoria began to fade when I focused on a very prominent word in the e-mail I had received from the editor: DEADLINE. Now it was time to come back down to Earth and get serious; I had a deadline to meet! Over the years, I've learned not to fear deadlines, but to meet them head on.

If you've got deadlines, first rid yourself of guilt. The first step in meeting a deadline is giving yourself permission to focus on something that's just for you. Having your own interests and goals makes you a happier person and, in turn, a better mother, daughter, sister, or friend. I often make a deal with myself; if I can complete a household chore or two, then I am free to spend some time in my studio. Once there, I approach my mixed-media and collage work in stages. I create each piece a step at a time; often the drying time between each stage equates to time for chores, phone calls, e-mails, blog and website updates, or errands. I change hats frequently during the day, from mother to artist to homemaker and back again, and I even delegate some of the household tasks that I would ordinarily handle myself.

The second key is to stay organized! Prioritize everything that needs to be done each day, and make that to-do list your new best friend. There is no shame in carrying over to tomorrow something from today's list. Post your list in a prominent place to help you stay on task. If the project you've committed to is an article or essay, keep your journal out so the moment an idea strikes you can jot down a sentence or two. When the time comes to write, you'll have a loose outline of ideas. The portability of using a journal allows you to take it with you, and you may also find your words flow more easily from pen to paper rather than at the computer.

Never turn down an opportunity that comes your way, whether it's for a commission or an article. Just manage your time and tasks, stay organized, and eliminate guilt from your emotional repertoire. You'll meet every deadline and be glad you did!

Nancy Lefko, *Living the Artful Life*, 8" × 10" (20.5 × 25.5 cm). Dressmaker's tissue, ink, acrylic paint, and paper collage.

ART AND HEALING

by Christy Hydeck

Creativity is so central to my existence that I only recently began to consciously recognize its benefits as a healing tool. As a child, my arms violently flailed every which way, my legs kicked backward as I walked, and loud uncontrollable grunts emerged from my mouth, expressing what was later diagnosed as bipolar disorder, obsessive-compulsive disorder, and Tourette's syndrome. I found my only refuge within acts of creativity.

I doodled. I colored outside the lines with reckless abandon. I created magical lands out of everyday things for my dolls. I wrote stories and immersed myself in playing the piano. I cut up books and made cards for loved ones. To my parents' dismay, I began taping words from magazines to my bedroom walls, stapling photos, sketching and spray-painting quotes, lyrics, and poetry. The walls evolved as I did, and bore every emotion I experienced. It was

Above: Christy Hydeck, *Move Among Mysteries*: 8" × 10" (20.5 × 25.5 cm). Altered photo.

Left: Christy Hydeck, *Spoken of the Soul*. 8" × 10" (20.5 × 25.5 cm). Altered photo.

my shrine, my sanctuary, my visual diary. It was the place where I discovered my personal truths and found my solace.

The act of creating can be transformational. Much fuss is made about the benefits of visualization, but I propose that art offers us something even greater. It is a transformational process that affects our every single way of being, seeing, and doing. Even the smallest acts of creativity can change our physiology and take us from a stressed state to a relaxed one. For me, the stroke of a brush, the stimulation of colors with design, and the act of carrying it all out gives me a voice that words alone cannot.

I create daily. Yes, daily. Every single day for as far back as I can remember, I make the time to honor that part of myself. Not everything I create will hold some deep spiritual meaning or provide a particular personal insight to me, nor should it. Sometimes, creating is nothing more than an enjoyable activity that I gain pleasure from. It's the process that heals, the process that both soothes and invigorates, the process that is a reflection of my soul, my heart, and my mind. It captivates me.

Personally, developing backgrounds is what I find to be the most therapeutic. I try not to get too wrapped up in the final product because I never want to lose sight of the all-important process. *Cut ... tear ... glue ... add a layer ... remove some paint ... need more paint ... try something new ... stamp here ... add texture here ... wipe off there ... paint to the rhythm of the music ... transfer here ... oops ... here too ...* You get the idea.

Christy Hydeck, *Soul's Estate*.
8" × 10" (20.5 × 25.5 cm). Altered photo.

My process is an accurate reflection of my life. I look past first impressions and find what lies beneath. I find it exciting, sometimes scary, and often eye-opening. Any sense of stability I possess is a testament to the sheer power creativity offers. Creating art provides an acceptable outlet for the larger-than-life thoughts that overpower my hectic, unquiet mind. It drives me and lessens the pain of depression.

MY PROCESS IS AN ACCURATE REFLECTION OF MY LIFE.

I challenge you to become conscious of the healing properties of creativity. Find the outlet that works best for you, whether it's a journal, a canvas, pounding clay, creating an assemblage, or something else. Art will guide you through the gravest of times and will always offer you a safe, comforting place to escape to.

NONE OF YOUR BEESWAX COLLAGE

I love the look of beeswax. It gives a soft, dreamy aspect to artwork, as if you were peering at it through an old bottle. Unfortunately, you can't apply beeswax over acrylic paint, and you have to use it on a rigid substrate. I've come up with Busy Beeswax, an alternative solution that mimics the look of wax without the restrictions. You can embed objects in Busy Beeswax, and it can be applied over acrylics, stamped, layered, and used on canvas; no heat is needed, and you don't have to worry about fumes, allowing for even more art therapy with less stress!

MATERIALS

- Prepared background (see page 21), 5" × 7" (12.5 × 18 cm)
- Fluid acrylic paints in your choice of colors
- Objects to embed, such as dried flowers
- Golden Extra Heavy Gel Medium (semigloss)
- Golden Fluid acrylic paints: iridescent gold deep (fine), transparent yellow iron oxide, iridescent bright gold (fine)
- Graphite pencil

TOOLS

- Paintbrushes
- Jar with lid for mixing Busy Beeswax
- Palette knife
- Stylus and/or stamp of your choice
- Baby wipes
- Chamois cloth

Pam Carriker, *None of Your Beeswax.*
5" × 7" (12.5 × 18 cm). Encaustic and mixed-media collage.

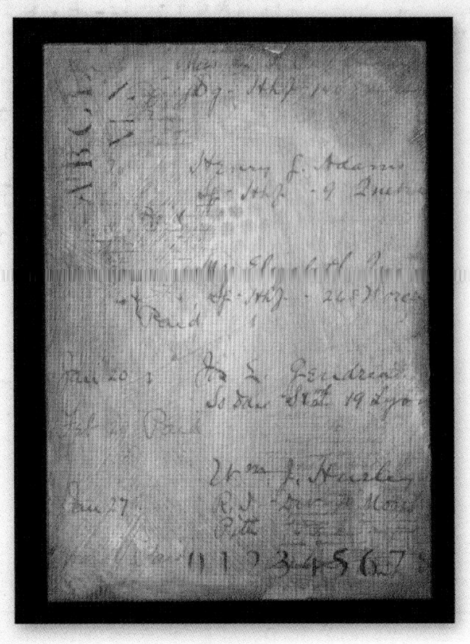

FIG. 1

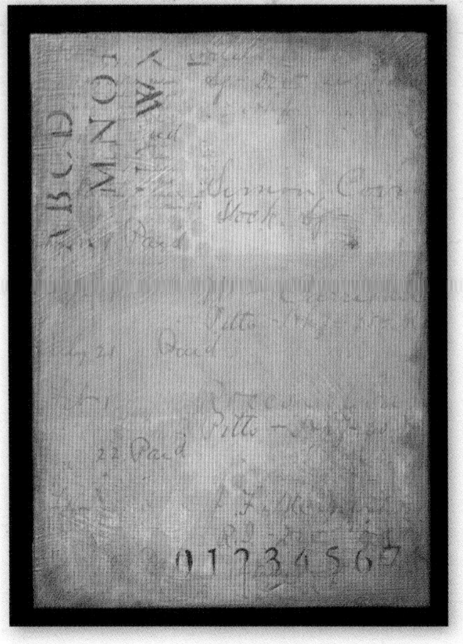

FIG. 2

FIG. 3

1 Choose a background from your premade stash or prepare a background (**Figure 1**).

2 Paint a portion of the background with a wash of one part fluid acrylic paint and one part water in a color that contrasts with the background. Let dry (**Figure 2**).

3 Lay out objects you wish to embed and move them around until you get an arrangement you like. Set them aside.

4 To make Busy Beeswax, mix in the jar until completely combined:

- 4 tablespoons Golden Extra Heavy Gel Medium (semigloss)
- 1 drop iridescent gold deep (fine) paint
- 2 drops transparent yellow iron oxide paint
- 1 drop iridescent bright gold (fine) paint

Using the palette knife, apply the "beeswax" mixture using smooth strokes from top to bottom. While the mixture is still wet, lay the objects in place and gently pat so they'll hold. Let dry thoroughly. Cover any remaining Busy Beeswax mixture so it won't dry out (**Figure 3**).

5 Add another layer of Busy Beeswax and let dry.

6 Add additional paint details such as dots. Enhance these details with a graphite pencil (**Figure 4**).

7 Add a final coat of the Busy Beeswax paint mixture with the palette knife. Wet your finger and smooth out any ridges with a circular motion, rewetting your finger as needed (**Figure 5**).

8 Use a stylus or an awl to scratch in a word or stamp in a detail, being sure to pull the stamp straight up to keep the design intact. Wash your tools off immediately and let the artwork dry.

FIG. 4

FIG. 5

9 Dilute a dark color of paint with water. Rub over the stylus or stamp detail and wipe off the surface with baby wipes, leaving paint in the grooves.

10 Enhance the sheen by buffing with a chamois cloth.

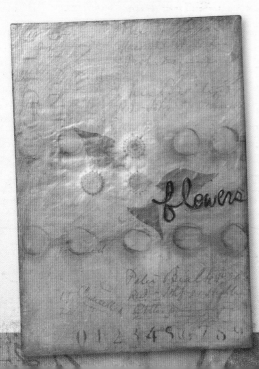

SEVEN-DAY JOURNAL

DAY 4: RESIST TECHNIQUES

Using products you already have in new ways is not only economical, but it can also open up a whole new side to your creative experience. Here are several methods you can use to make resists, treatments that keep some areas of the page from accepting paint. You'll create amazing effects with everyday mediums.

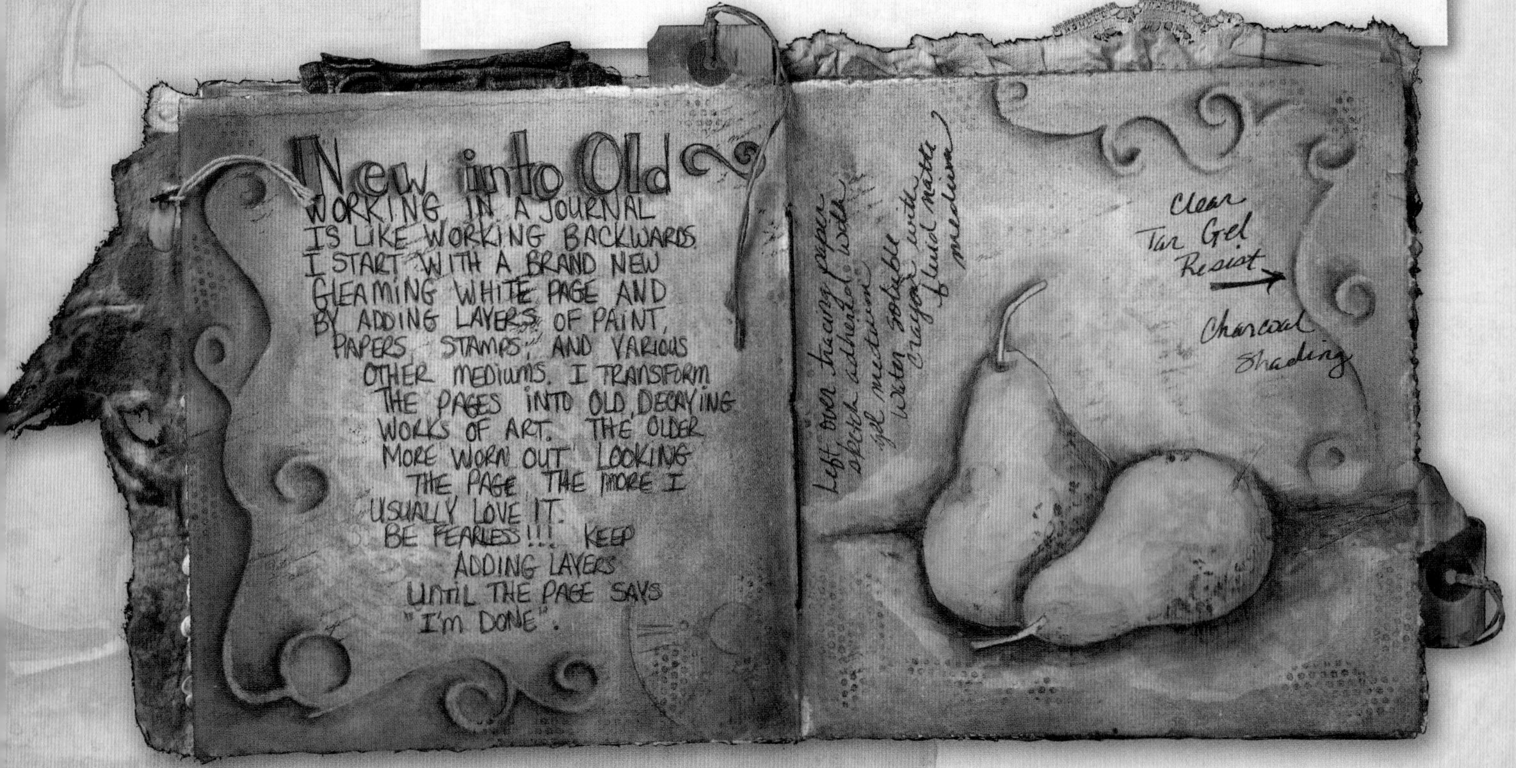

New into Old
WORKING IN A JOURNAL IS LIKE WORKING BACKWARDS. I START WITH A BRAND NEW GLEAMING WHITE PAGE AND BY ADDING LAYERS OF PAINT, PAPERS STAMPS, AND VARIOUS OTHER MEDIUMS. I TRANSFORM THE PAGES INTO OLD, DECAYING WORKS OF ART. THE OLDER MORE WORN OUT LOOKING THE PAGE THE MORE I USUALLY LOVE IT. BE FEARLESS!!! KEEP ADDING LAYERS UNTIL THE PAGE SAYS "I'M DONE".
Left over tracing paper sketch adhered with gel medium
Water soluble crayon with fluid matte medium
Clear Tar Gel Resist
Charcoal Shading

GESSO RESIST

Gesso is a staple in any mixed-media studio. Generally used for prepping canvas and other substrates to accept various mediums, it can also be used as a resist. Choose white, black, or clear gesso and experiment for a variety of looks.

MATERIALS

- Gesso
- Journal page with prepared background from Seven-Day Journal (page 26)
- Fluid acrylic paints

TOOLS

- Foam paint stamps
- Sponge brush
- Paintbrush
- Rag

1 Apply gesso to a stamp or other texture tool using an inexpensive sponge brush. Stamp the gesso onto your page. Wash the stamp in soapy water immediately; do not allow gesso to dry on the stamp. Allow gesso on the page to dry.

2 Use a paintbrush to paint a thin wash of acrylic paint right over the gesso. Follow with a rag to wipe off the gessoed areas. The rag will pick up most of the paint from the gessoed areas.

3 To achieve more texture, generously pat gesso onto a foam paint stamp. Stamp onto your work, pulling the stamp straight up for raised texture, smooshing it from side to side for a slightly distorted shape, or creating a series of fading images by applying gesso to the stamp once and stamping several times.

Pam Carriker, *Seven-Day Journal*.
8" × 8" (20.5 × 20.5 cm) closed. Handmade journal with mixed-media pages.

CRAYON RESIST

Good old wax crayons, just like the ones you used in grade school, can create a fun look on your page. By randomly doodling, scratching lines onto your page, and then painting over them or making a rubbing with them, it's easy to find that artistic inner child you thought you'd left in first grade.

MATERIALS

- Wax crayons
- Journal page from Seven-Day Journal with prepared background (page 26)
- Fluid acrylic paints

TOOLS

- Paintbrush
- Paper towels
- Baby wipes
- Iron and/or heat gun (optional)

1 Using any color of crayon, make marks on a page with a prepared acrylic painted background.

2 Paint a wash of paint over the crayon markings and wipe off the paint with a damp paper towel or baby wipe.

3 Change the look by layering different colors or coloring more heavily in some areas than others.

4 If you like, try removing the crayon after you've painted over it and the paint has dried. Simply lay a paper towel over the crayon and press with a warm iron for a couple of seconds, allowing the crayon to soak into the paper towel.

5 You can also change the appearance of the crayon by heating the crayoned areas with a heat gun to give a glossy appearance.

CHAPTER 5

THE WORKING ARTIST

It can be hard to make your mark as an artist while working full-time, especially if your day job isn't related to anything resembling art. I've been a stay-at-home mom and a working gal, so I know from experience that time management applies to both sides of the fence. Just as a woman who stays at home battles for time for herself, so do those who work all day and come home to a long list of pesky chores. The grass may seem greener on the other side, but by fertilizing the lawn under your own two feet you can achieve things you never thought possible. So kick off your shoes and run barefoot through the meadows. Just make sure you do it on your lunch hour!

> **THE GRASS MAY SEEM GREENER ON THE OTHER SIDE, BUT BY FERTILIZING THE LAWN UNDER YOUR OWN TWO FEET YOU CAN ACHIEVE THINGS YOU NEVER THOUGHT POSSIBLE.**

This chapter will help you to bridge the gap between your day job and your art. The *Artist Spotlight* assemblage project by Seth Apter will show you how disparate objects can work in harmony, just as your varied roles can harmonize into a rich life. My *Speed of Life* version takes an already-prepared background to create a unique piece of assembled art with steps that can fit into small blocks of available time. In the ongoing *Seven-Day Journal* project, we add stamping and masking off parts of the page to create layers of color and texture.

ART IS NEVER FINISHED.
ONLY ABANDONED.
—LEONARDO DA VINCI

BRINGING HOME THE BACON AND FRYING IT UP IN A PAN

When I first began to dream of writing a book about art, I was working full time and painting in my spare time. I was married but hadn't yet had children, so I did have some evenings to devote to art. I had a wonderful group of artistic friends, and we all loved finding ways to be

Pam Carriker, *The Promise of Life.*
8" × 8" (20.5 × 20.5 cm). Mixed-media collage with acrylic paint.

creative. We all worked, but we found time for our art because we wanted to!

Then, as they always do, things changed. We started families and the free time we had turned into family time. My desire to create turned to creating for my family. I was still creating, just with a different focus.

Sometimes all you need is a different focus to make creativity fit into your daily life. Give yourself credit for the creative things you do accomplish. I'm betting there are many creative things that you do right now that don't fit the traditional idea of art. It's a great journal exercise to write them down and find ways to expand on them. Recognize the creative beast that resides within and let it out! Praise it for the things it already accomplishes and help it to find even more ways to romp and play!

It's your outlook on your life that is key to living it the way you desire. Next time you feel frustrated by the hectic, uncreative life you think you're living, take a minute and pat yourself on the back for those creative moments that did happen, because they do happen— each and every day. So whether you bring home the bacon or fry it up in a pan, celebrate creative moments each and every day.

MAKE A PLAYDATE (WITH YOURSELF)

I was sitting next to my eight-year-old son on an airplane as we both worked in our art journals. He began his page with some interesting circles and wavy lines as I watched out of the corner of my eye and worked on a page background in my own journal. He said, "I'm going to draw what I see out the window and then make it into something else," and he proceeded to do just that. He had no fears about making those first marks on the blank page, no worries of what he should do, and no expectations about the outcome. He simply created.

I marveled at the differences in our approaches to the same journal page. My journal is a place to try and reach the artistic vision that he begins with. Although it can take several minutes or more for me to loosen up and play, he starts out that way, just pencil to paper. Somewhere along the path of life, we seem to lose that natural tendency to create just for the sheer joy of the process. Art becomes serious or we put it away altogether. Our journey as artists is to find our way back to that special place and nurture it on a regular basis.

Pam Carriker, *Without Wings*. 8" × 10" (20.5 × 25.5 cm). Mixed-media collage with acrylic paint, paper, charcoal, and water-soluble crayon.

When you lose your way, it can take some work to find the inner child that dwells in your artistic soul, but it's a necessity to reach your creative potential. It takes a conscious effort to arrange time to be creative. Scheduling time to play is okay. It's not something to feel guilty about. It helps you unlock the mystery of yourself, and it's much more fun and cheaper than therapy! It helps to write creative time down on the calendar—this forces you to make a decision when something else threatens to take over the time allotted for art. Write it in pen so you can't erase it!

> IT CAN TAKE SOME WORK TO FIND THE INNER CHILD THAT DWELLS IN YOUR ARTISTIC SOUL, BUT IT'S A NECESSITY TO REACH YOUR CREATIVE POTENTIAL.

I'M NOT GIVING UP MY DAY JOB  (YET)!

by Jodi Uhl

Jodi Ohl, *Banker Chick*. 9" × 12" (23 × 30.5 cm). Collage and acrylic paint on canvas.

As much as I'd like to resign and start packing up my office today, I'm not in a position to do so—yet. I've never been one to jump off a cliff just because it seems like a good idea. Oh, I know others do it every day, but I need to plan, so for the last couple of years I've been getting my house in order so I can live my dream. Will there ever be a right time? If you're determined, you do what you must. I intend to do this with my art. The stars don't have to align before I go full time, but I need to feel they're in the best position possible before I take flight. Here are some of the things I'm doing to prepare for that day.

1 Develop a Business Plan

Yes, if you're going to be a full-time artist, you need a road map for your business. It's no different than starting a restaurant or shop. Creating art all day long is great, but you need a plan to develop a customer base—not just an art plan, but also a business plan, with projections for sales and profit margins, ideas for retail outlets, a strategy for marketing, and more.

2 Excel in Time Management

Organizational skills are critical. I list priorities, ideas, and schedules. These don't have to be restrictive, down-to-the-minute plans, but you should be able to establish deadlines for your production, marketing, listing, and networking obligations. Successful people can be counted on to get the job done. You're more likely to succeed with a plan than if you leave it all to chance.

3 Prepare Financially and Understand Pricing

How much do you want to earn with your business? Do you know how much you'd have to create in order to achieve this goal? Figure it out. I sell quite well with my items in the $25 to $40 range, but I can't sell enough work at that price point to be solvent. I've decided to do larger pieces as well as branch out into prints, write articles, attend shows, teach, and expand my presence in galleries and local stores. Create a budget with an eye toward a rainy day. We all know it'll come. If you can't survive one, think twice about spending all your creative loot at the supply store each time you successfully sell some of your art. Open up a savings or separate business account so you can prepare for seasonal slowdowns. Pricing is a touchy subject, and I have no magic formula. Just remember—you're worth it. Price your work to include not only the cost of supplies and labor but also hidden expenses such as taxes, insurance, fees, and shipping. Oh, and profit, yes, profit!

4 Marketing

We'd all like to subscribe to the "Make it, and they will come," theory, but it doesn't just happen. There are a lot of ways to get your name into the world, and you just need to find what works for you. The Internet affords so many opportunities to the modern artist; there's never been a better time to be one. You can sell an item from your Smalltown, USA, living room to someone in Smalltown, New Zealand, without ever leaving your house!

Do your best and don't give up. Everything is a balancing act; there's no denying that. We all need dreams, and belief in them can be magical. However, for dreams to come true, we must align our own stars. Starting with a plan will make it happen with fewer unexpected detours. Although I haven't quit my day job yet, I know that day is coming, and when it does, I'll be ready for it!

Jodi Ohl, *Art Chick*. 6" × 12" (15 × 30.5 cm). Collage and acrylic paint on canvas.

ASSEMBLING ART

by Seth Apter

I often use materials and images that I gather on my travels in layered assemblage projects. Layers are the driving force behind much of my artwork, in part for the visual impact they create. Assemblage also inspires me on a metaphorical level. The process of building an assemblage, or any artwork that has multiple layers, allows us to re-create the layers that make us who we are. In doing so, we build a sense of history, substance, and meaning into the work.

MATERIALS

- Book boards or four vintage book covers cut to 7½" × 5⅛", 5⅝" × 3¼", 8½" × 5½", 8½" × 5½" [19 × 13 cm, 14.3 × 8.5 cm, 21.5 × 14 cm, 21.5 × 14 cm])
- Glue suitable for collage
- Vintage book pages and assorted papers
- Gesso
- Amber shellac
- Calligraphy inks: brown and black
- Distress Ink pads: Black Soot, Antique Linen, Old Paper, Tea Dye
- Gold-leafing pen
- Fabric scraps
- Papyrus paper, 2" × 3" (5 × 7.5 cm)
- Found strips of metal, metal letter X, metal filigree, distressed metal stars, metal diamond shapes, and other flat metal shapes
- Brads and mini brads
- Vintage wooden face
- Flexible wire, 10" (25.5 cm)
- Found wood strip, about 6" (15 cm)
- Vintage metal file tab

TOOLS

- Masking tape
- Texturizing tools such as straightedge, corrugated cardboard, netting
- Paintbrushes
- Sponge brush
- Eyelets and eyelet setter
- Sanding block
- Hole punch or awl
- Dremel tool

Seth Apter, *Assemblage.*
6" × 9" (15 × 23 cm). Mixed-media assemblage.

FIG. 1   **FIG. 2**   **FIG. 3**   **FIG. 4**

1 Lay the 7½" × 5⅛" (19 × 13 cm) book board on your work surface. This will become the middle of three stacked book boards.

2 Glue vintage book pages (mine came from a French dictionary) onto the book board. Let dry. Distress the edges of the piece by applying a strip of masking tape to the edge of the glued page and pulling it off **(Figure 1)**.

3 Cover the piece with gesso, allowing text from the page to show through. Immediately, while the gesso is still wet, texturize the gesso using a straightedge, corrugated cardboard, netting, and the point of a paintbrush. Leave the edges of the piece only partially covered with gesso so that a border will be created in upcoming steps **(Figure 2)**.

4 Once the gesso is dry, sponge on amber shellac with the sponge brush. Allow to dry. Sponge on a second coat **(Figure 3)**.

5 Splatter the piece with amber shellac and with brown and black calligraphy ink by dipping a paintbrush into the ink and tapping the brush handle with another brush. Blend in dye ink such

as Distress Ink Black Soot around the edges of the front surface and sparingly on the face of the surface to age the piece. Punch holes for eyelets in all four corners and attach hand-distressed eyelets (distress them by hammering, sanding, adding paint, or otherwise adding texture and character). Edge the sides of the book board with the gold-leafing pen **(Figure 4)**.

6 Lay the 5⅝" × 3¼" (14.25 × 8.5 cm) book board on your work surface. This will become the top layer of the three stacked book boards.

7 Glue scraps of decorative paper onto the book board. Distress the surface and edges with the sanding block. Blend in dye inks such as Distress Ink Black Soot and Antique Linen around the edges of the front surface and sparingly on the face of the surface to age the piece. Edge the sides of the book board with the gold-leafing pen. Glue two overlapping torn fabric remnants to the back of the book board so the fabric is partially revealed **(Figure 5)**.

8 Cut a small piece of papyrus paper and glue it to the center of the book board. Cut a piece of vintage paper with script, aged with dye ink such as Distress Ink Black Soot, Antique Linen, Old Paper,

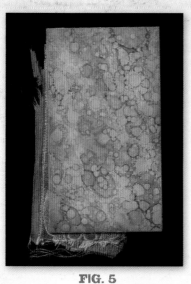

FIG. 5

FIG. 6

FIG. 7

or Tea Dye. Glue it to the upper book board. Cut and distress the found metal strip and glue it to the middle book board **(Figure 6)**.

9 Glue a hand-distressed metal X over the paper with script. Punch two holes at the inner part of the X and add two brads. Glue a second smaller piece of found metal strip in the center of the strip at the bottom of the book board. Punch holes in the bottom center of the book board and attach found metal pieces with mini brads **(Figure 7)**.

10 Glue a small metal filigreed piece to the center of the X at the top of the book board.

11 Glue a flat, oddly shaped, rusted metal piece to the center of the papyrus paper. Glue the vintage wooden face to the rusted metal piece. Punch two small holes on each side of the face and attach it to the smallest book board piece with wire.

12 Glue the top book board to the center of the middle book board.

13 Use the 8½" × 5½" (21.5 × 14 cm) book board as the bottom of the stack. Glue the middle book board to the bottom book board, leaving about ⅞" (2.2 cm) at the top.

14 Drill four holes with the Dremel tool into the book board using the eyelets in the middle book board as a guide. Thread metal wire through all four holes, creating a border on the middle book board.

15 Glue onto the top book board the distressed metal stars in the upper corner and the found wood strip in the upper center. Glue the distressed found metal strip in the center of the wood strip.

16 Glue the diamond-shaped metal piece to the upper center of the middle book board so that it extends above the center of the wood strip at the top.

17 Add vintage paper with script, aged with dye ink such as Distress Ink Black Soot, Antique Linen, Old Paper, or Tea Dye, to a vintage metal file tab. Glue the file tab to the back of the book cover in the upper center. Cover the back of the piece with a second 8½" × 5½" (21.5 × 14 cm) book cover.

FROM THE DESK OF SHARON TOMLINSON

by Sharon Tomlinson

Even though I work full time, I find time and space to make lots of beautiful and satisfying art. In part, I do this by making art right at my desk—my office desk. As my own boss, it's fairly easy for me to integrate art making into my business, but even if you work for someone else, you might find my tips helpful.

At my office, I keep an oil pastel set handy right beside the telephone. Art from my desk started out with doodling on my appointment calendar and sharing it on my blog each Friday. I then began keeping an inspiration journal, where I glue assorted sketches, quotes, and thoughts on anything I want to keep and remember.

As my art-at-my-desk practice evolved, I began to pack an art bag with limited supplies for whatever I might be working on. The bag always carries the current masterpiece in progress. Some days I never manage to even open the art bag, but I never leave it at home—there might be a moment for art. At the very least, I can spend time staring at the masterpiece in progress, an important stage that keeps me ready when the art moment arrives.

Eventually, I began to bring art supplies to the office to stay. If I have duplicate supplies, I keep one at home and one at the office. I keep scissors, cutting mat and knives, brushes, art pins, and even a small light box in my office art studio—and yes, at this point I can call it that!

I like to make mail art at my office desk. I keep a plastic bag for used postage stamps for collage; that's just one of the art supplies my office offers up. I save security envelopes and am amazed at how many different designs there are. Painting on old file folders is fun—I use them for hand-bound journal covers.

> **ART FROM MY DESK STARTED OUT WITH DOODLING ON MY APPOINTMENT CALENDAR AND SHARING IT ON MY BLOG EACH FRIDAY.**

If you can make a little time at work, and keep a stash of supplies at your desk, you, too, will find many ways to send art from your own desk and keep the creative flame burning while you're away from home.

Sharon Tomlinson, *Expecting Wings*. 8" × 8" (20.5 × 20.5 cm). Mixed-media collage on canvas.

ASSEMBLED ANTHOLOGY

Just as we assemble a life that includes work and art, we can assemble art that is dimensional and visually appealing. Mixed-media artists are notorious for hoarding all sorts of found objects and many are just as notorious for finding them too special to part with! But the reward for doing so is a successful work of art. For this project, I chose a 12" × 12" × 2" (30.5 × 30.5 × 5 cm) canvas from my stash of prepared backgrounds, then attached a smaller canvas board substrate prepared with my foolproof crackle method and some additional vintage hardware to transform the canvas in no time at all.

MATERIALS

- Paper-backed canvas board panel, 8" × 8" (20.5 × 20.5 cm)
- Black gesso
- White glue, such as Elmer's school glue
- Heavy-body acrylic paints: Titan buff, a dark contrasting color, and additional colors of your choice
- Assorted fluid acrylic paints, including burnt umber
- Acrylic satin-finish glazing medium
- Jewelry or gift box, 2" × 3" (5 × 7.5 cm)
- Graphite pencil
- Cloth tape
- Molding paste
- Canvas with prepared background, 12" × 12" × 2" (30.5 × 30.5 × 5 cm)
- White gel pen
- Charcoal pencil
- Assorted vintage metal findings with interesting shapes, such as old drawer pulls and doorknob parts
- 22-gauge craft wire, 36" (91.5 cm) long
- Assorted brads and nails
- Heavy gel medium
- Bits of text clipped from old books

TOOLS

- Palette knife
- 2" (5 cm) chip brush
- Assorted paintbrushes
- Old toothbrush
- X-acto knife
- Hole-punching tool, such as a Crop-A-Dile
- Paper towels
- Hammer
- Wire cutters

Pam Carriker, *Assembled Anthology*. 12" × 12" × 2" (30.5 × 30.5 × 5 cm). Mixed-media assemblage on canvas.

FIG. 1   FIG. 2   FIG. 3

1 Cover the front of the paper-backed canvas board panel with black gesso using a palette knife to achieve a nice texture. Be sure to cover the edges as well to finish them off. Let dry and then use the chip brush to cover the back with gesso to prevent warping (**Figure 1**).

2 To make the crackle surface, use the chip brush to paint white glue onto the whole background. Paint in one direction only, making the glue thicker in some areas than others. The size of the crackle will depend on the amount of glue applied in this step. The thicker the glue, the larger the cracks.

3 While the glue is still wet, use a palette knife to apply Titan buff heavy-body acrylic paint. Go in one direction, laying the paint on the substrate in a smooth motion, from top to bottom. Don't overwork the paint, just lay it down in one stroke. Let this dry thoroughly and watch the cracks develop as it dries.

4 Mix an acrylic glaze of one part titan buff paint, two parts water, and one-half part acrylic glazing medium. Brush the mixture around all edges of the paper-backed canvas board, feathering it in to create an aged border around the entire piece (**Figure 2**).

5 Mix some of the contrasting dark acrylic paint with water to create an inky consistency. Pick it up with an old toothbrush and add some spatters by running your thumb across the bristles.

6 Trace the outline of the small jewelry/gift box onto the desired location on the canvas board with the graphite pencil. Using an X-acto knife, cut out the rectangle you've traced. Insert the small box into the hole made in step 6 and use cloth tape applied to the back to hold it in place (**Figure 3**).

7 Use a palette knife to apply molding paste to the inside of the box, covering any small crack between the canvas board and the box. Let dry and paint the inside of the box as desired.

8 Using a hole-punching tool such as a Crop-A-Dile, punch a hole in each corner of the canvas board. Paint the inside of the holes with black gesso.

9 On the 12" × 12" (30.5 × 30.5 cm) canvas, add white glue to parts of the canvas using a palette knife and follow with a layer of heavy-body acrylic paint in a color of your choice applied in the same way (**Figures 4 and 5**). Allow to dry; the paint will crackle.

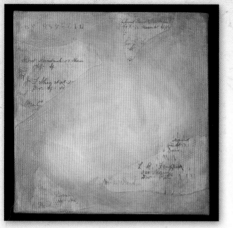

FIG. 4

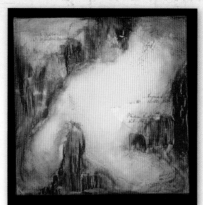

FIG. 5

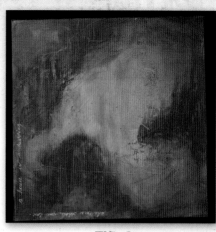

FIG. 6

10 Mix a glaze with 3 tablespoons acrylic glazing medium and two or three drops of burnt umber fluid acrylic. Apply the glaze to the entire canvas, wiping off the excess as needed with a paper towel **(Figure 6)**.

11 Add touches of acrylic paint in a color that ties it in with the canvas board. Using a white gel pen, journal text around the edge of the canvas. Use a charcoal pencil to shade where desired.

12 Attach vintage metal findings to the canvas board using wire, brads, and nails, as needed. Hammer a nail into each corner of the base canvas, leaving the head sticking up a bit.

13 Use four 8" (20.5 cm) pieces of wire to attach the canvas board to the base canvas, threading each wire through one of the holes and wrapping it around the nail heads. Further secure by adding heavy gel medium to the back of the box and adhering it to the canvas.

14 Add pieces of text to box or elsewhere on the canvas board using heavy gel medium to glue them down.

ASSEMBLAGE

Creating an assemblage is like writing a story using found objects to invite the viewer in and unearth their meaning.

Some tips:
- Identify a word or two that expresses the theme of your work before you begin.
- Keeping your theme in mind, find several objects that represent what you want to convey.
- Choose additional elements with textures or shapes that enhance the visual appearance of your work. Lay all of the elements out on your worktable and spend some time positioning them on the canvas until you achieve a simple composition that reflects the theme.
- It is not necessary to use every item; pick and choose key elements that will convey your message simply.
- Attach the items in various ways to add interest to the piece.
- Take a break from your work and look at it with fresh eyes to see whether your message is coming through.
- A few well-chosen pieces make a bolder statement than using too many.

SEVEN-DAY JOURNAL
DAY 5: STAMP AND MASK

By now, your Seven-Day Journal should be taking on a life of its own and be full of color and inspiration. Stamping and masking are two easy ways to add even more depth, color, texture, and interest to your art journal pages. Although there are beautiful readymade stamps available, it's easy to stamp with found objects—soon you'll be eyeing everything for stamping potential!

STAMPING

Carving your own stamps is a great way to put your personal touch on your journal pages, but it's time-consuming. Use things you already have to get a personalized look in less time. In addition to direct stamping, try making a collographic stamping tool by gluing cardboard shapes and other textural elements to a cardboard base.

MATERIALS

- Permanent ink pads
- Journal page from Seven-Day Journal with prepared background (page 26)

TOOLS

- Foam stamps
- Sandpaper
- X-acto knife
- Awl
- Rubber stamps
- Found object stamping tools such as caps and lids, pencil erasers, rubber bands wrapped around a brayer, corks, Lego toys, bubble wrap

1 Distress inexpensive foam stamps using sandpaper, an X-acto knife, an awl, or other tools. Mark up the stamps to create your own look.

2 Using the ink pads, stamp the journal pages with the distressed stamps, rubber stamps, and found objects.

3 Try imperfectly inking some of the stamps so that only part of the stamped image prints.

MASKING

Masking off areas of the page and then painting or inking the page creates a soft look that allows underlying layers to show through. Anything that covers up a portion of your page can act as a mask, from a piece of removable tape to a readymade masking liquid. Here are some easy ways to create masks at little or no cost.

MATERIALS

- Ink pads
- Plain scrap paper
- Journal page from Seven-Day Journal with prepared background (page 26)
- Fluid acrylic paint in your choice of color(s)
- Removable blue painter's tape
- Clear contact paper

TOOLS

- Rubber stamps
- Small scissors
- X-acto knife
- Cutting mat
- Paintbrush
- Fine-tip permanent marker

MASK

1 Using the ink pads and rubber stamps, stamp an image onto the scrap paper, painter's tape, or clear contact paper.

2 Cut the image out using scissors or an X-acto knife on the cutting mat.

3 Place the image on your journal page and ink or paint over it to leave a silhouette of the shape. If you like, stamp directly on the same page with the stamp.

Pam Carriker, *Seven-Day Journal.*
8" × 8" (20.5 × 20.5 cm) closed.
Handmade journal with mixed-media pages.

CHAPTER 6

ART ON THE GO

You ALREADY have everything inside of you To BE an ARTIST. YOU are an artist NOW Feel it. KNOW it. BELIEVE IT. BE IT.

an object found

TIME STAYS LONG ENOUGH FOR ANYONE WHO WILL USE IT.
—LEONARDO DA VINCI

Have art, will travel! Leave home without your most cherished art supplies with the thought of not creating for days? No way. Some of the best inspiration comes from traveling and seeing new things, so whenever you have the chance to take off, capitalize on the moment. You'll be amazed at the creative opportunities that appear when you're tuned in to them. You may even start to hope you find yourself waiting for a delayed flight or a doctor who's running late! Personalize a traveling art kit so you have art supplies at your fingertips at any time. Keep your kit close by so you never have to let idle minutes tick by. It's not enough just to make more time; you have to make the most from the time you already have.

In this chapter's projects, we make the most of photos, since that's what many travelers bring home. Lisa Bebi's paint-over technique shows you how to create on top of photos while my *Speed of Life* version looks at creating from the bottom up. Using an already-prepared background gives you a jumpstart on either project. When you head out the door, take along your art kit and your journal from the *Seven-Day Journal* project. It's time to add words to the mix, making this an on-the-go project.

SOME OF THE BEST INSPIRATION COMES FROM TRAVELING AND SEEING NEW THINGS, SO WHENEVER YOU HAVE THE CHANCE TO TAKE OFF, CAPITALIZE ON THE MOMENT.

Art Credits: page 143

the road less traveled

Contemplation

if i could fly

Ramber09

MARRY ME, FLY FOR FREE!
(SOME RESTRICTIONS APPLY)

My husband is a commercial pilot, so we fly for free—but we travel standby, and let me tell you, sometimes we stand by for hours! My art journal is my sanity, turning unproductive, wasted time into coveted, no distractions, no excuses, quality time to bury myself in my own thoughts and creativity.

To make the most of otherwise unproductive time away from the studio, have several pages in your art journal partially done before leaving home. I always have pages in varying stages of completion, so it's easy to pick up a journal and add to those pages while I'm away from my studio.

While traveling I add collage fodder found along the way or simply write about the trip itself. Look around you and use the things you see. Everything is fair game for journaling! Here are some examples of things you can incorporate into your pages:

- ticket stubs
- restaurant or airplane napkins
- newspaper text
- clean food or candy wrappers
- receipts from terminal stores
- trip itinerary
- magazine images

Try these ideas, too:

- journal about current events from television news feeds in waiting areas
- draw what you see: tray table with airline food, the cover of a book, your luggage, your sunglasses—these sketches are snapshots of your day and a great exercise for your art muscles
- use coffee stirrers to make straight edges or an interesting shape to trace around for journaling text inside the shape.

FLYING WITHOUT FEATHERS IS NOT EASY: MY WINGS HAVE NO FEATHERS.
—TITUS MACCIUS PLAUTUS

TIP: FLIGHT DELAYED!

- Run out of prepared backgrounds? I've purposely spilled coffee to stain my pages when I ran out of prepped backgrounds! It opens up the scope of your creativity when you're forced to use only what's around you. Stretch that creative muscle and you'll make the most of creative time away from home.

Pam Carriker, *If I Could Fly*. 9" × 12" (23 × 30.5 cm). Acrylic paint and collage on watercolor paper.

THE ESSENTIAL FIVE:
AN ARTIST'S SURVIVAL GUIDE

What are the must-have tools to take along when you are away? These vary from artist to artist, but a few guidelines will help you select your own kit of five essential traveling art supplies. Ask yourself which five art supplies you'd want with you on a desert island to help choose. Everyone can identify with being away from home, whether it's an overseas journey or being stuck in the dentist's waiting room. Having basic art supplies with you turns that wasted time into productive, creative time. What a positive boost to your frame of mind something as simple as this can bring. It can make your whole day! Whatever your style of travel, don't leave art behind—take it with you and enjoy every minute of the journey.

CREATE YOUR OWN ESSENTIAL FIVE

1 *Drawing tool.* What's your favorite drawing pencil? It's the one you always reach for. You really only need to take one with you. Mine is a woodless graphite pencil because of its smoothness, weight, and large workable area that makes it great for shading as well as drawing. Fill in your own favorite drawing tool below.

_____

2 *Adhesive.* This can be a sticky business! Think about portability, ease of use, and quality of hold. I like a glue stick such as UHU. Apply the glue stick to both the image and the surface of a substrate for good adhesion.

_____

3 *Eraser.* I use a kneaded eraser to blend, erase, and get interesting effects. An eraser is for more than just getting rid of mistakes; use yours to add special effects to your pages.

_____

4 *Color.* Sometimes this is my little travel-size watercolor set, sometimes water-soluble crayons, colored pencils, or colored markers. Whatever tools I decide to take, I usually take just a few of my favorite colors.

_____

5 *Pen.* Narrowing this down to one favorite pen is hard for me; sometimes I cheat and take more than one. Two basics are a fine-point permanent marker and a white gel pen.

_____

WHEN ONCE YOU HAVE TASTED FLIGHT,
YOU WILL FOREVER WALK THE EARTH
WITH YOUR EYES TURNED SKYWARD,
FOR THERE YOU HAVE BEEN, AND THERE
YOU WILL ALWAYS LONG TO RETURN.
—LEONARDO DA VINCI

LIVE BIG

by Suzi Blu

I am sitting on my boyfriend's dog-haired couch eating pizza and writing in a composition notebook. To me, this is living big. I have nothing and everything at the same time. Every day I do what I want. Yes, obligations—of course I have them. As I write, it's dark, it's snowing, and Gigi Rainbow Sparkle (a pint-size white Pekinese with googly eyes and missing front teeth) needs a walk. I can grumble and freeze and be miserable OR I can live big. Living big means celebrating small moments and making them events.

What is an event? It's an extraordinary occurrence. Give yourself permission to make small moments big. This might feel silly. For example, I'm walking Gigi at night, in the cold. Think of the ways I can make this activity a celebration! Think of all the things I could do to make me and my pooch comfortable. A thick wool hat and chunky gloves for me, Gigi dressed in a rainbow sweater with booties, chocolate chip cookies, or a cup of hot chocolate and pocket warmers.

Do you dare walk your dog on a neon leash that blinks? Or buy groceries in bunny slippers? How about wearing a tiara next time you make a deposit at the bank? I can tell you that when I do these things people smile. They do! Everyone is in a coma and bored and waiting for something fun to happen. They are waiting for YOU to make it happen. To live a big life means not waiting for someone to entertain you; instead, you become the entertainer. Yeah, they will laugh, but they will remember you, and as you live big and creatively, you give others the courage to live big and creatively, too.

Suzi Blu, *I Was a Boy Once*. 16" × 20" (40.5 × 51 cm). Acrylic paint on canvas.

So many people are sad and scared. By putting yourself out there you are creating a space where others can put themselves out there, too. Living big is about maintaining your sense of play and nurturing it. Maybe it's buying all the art supplies you want in one day and putting off the bills. Whatever it takes to make today the best day it can be, I say do it. Be a person with a big life. Next time you have something to do that you've done a thousand times and are so very bored, ask yourself, "How can I make this moment extraordinary? What would Suzi do?"

> **LIVING BIG IS ABOUT MAINTAINING YOUR SENSE OF PLAY AND NURTURING IT.**

THE CAREFREE PAINT-OVER TECHNIQUE

by Lisa Bebi

I am often in a hurry. To shortcut my work in the studio, I developed a technique of painting on top of photocopies of photos that come from my collection or my travels. Eventually, my technique of paint-over on a photocopy evolved further; as newer mediums and varnishes appeared on the market, I was able to treat the painting so that it is protected from ultraviolet light and resistant to scratches and unwanted marks.

MATERIALS

- Black-and-white photocopies
- Substrate
- Gel medium
- Fluid acrylic paints: nickel azo yellow, turquoise, bright pink, light blue, warm white

TOOLS

- Paintbrushes: wide, broad flat, fine

Lisa Bebi, *Untitled*. 8" × 10" (20.5 × 25.5 cm).
Paint and photocopy on cardboard.

FIG. 1

FIG. 2

FIG. 3

1 Choose an image with a simple subject and make a black-and-white inkjet copy, enlarging the image (**Figure 1**). I enlarged this photo by 160 percent (remember that enlarging an image operates in every direction; the image will increase 160 percent in width and 160 percent in height).

2 Glue the photocopy to your substrate using gel medium. Don't cover the inkjet image with medium; the plastic coating will prevent the paint from staining the paper in the next step. Using a wash of diluted nickel azo yellow paint and a wide paintbrush, stain the image and some of the foreground yellow. This adds an underlying warm glow to the painting (**Figure 2**).

3 With a broad flat brush, paint in turquoise over the background. This simplifies and flattens the background, creating a shallower, more two-dimensional working plane that helps focus the observer on the subject. Paint turquoise into the mid-tones of the subject, including skin and hair of people in the image (**Figure 3**).

4 Brush bright pink paint onto the skin of people in the image and in the upper right and lower left of the picture (**Figure 4**).

5 Redefine the background with a broad brush and a lighter blue color of acrylic paint by painting into the negative spaces around the subject.

6 Finally, use a fine brush to add a little warm white in washes on the skin and in some of the details to bring the piece to life.

FIG. 4

ART AT THE SPEED OF LIFE

A CREATIVE JOURNEY

by Lisa Kettell

Lisa Kettell, *Untitled*. 5" × 8" (12.5 × 20.5 cm).
Altered cigar box with cards.

I was just four years old when I received my first box of crayons and a coloring book, and my magical creative journey began. As I grew into adulthood, I promised myself that I would never stop believing in creativity and the existence of magic. After studying the fine arts in high school, I grew interested in illustration. It wasn't until college that I discovered collage. I loved the process of layering and altering surfaces while mixing in a variety of elements. I became a mixed-media artist.

Since then, I have explored many facets of the art world, and I think of myself as having a multifaceted muse who accompanies me on every journey that I embark on. Wherever I teach, wherever I visit, and whenever I create, my muse brings me my daily dose of creativity. I become the grand wizard of my work and turn my creative energy into magic for all to enjoy. Here are some of the ways that I work with the many sides of my imaginary muse.

> I BECOME THE GRAND WIZARD OF MY WORK AND TURN MY CREATIVE ENERGY INTO MAGIC FOR ALL TO ENJOY.

• **Create a book of inspiration.** Alter an old book and fill each page with a different art trend that inspires you. When you're stuck for motivation or inspiration, the pages will give you a push in the right creative direction. This is something you can take with you when you travel and continually add to when inspiration strikes.

• **Make your own success cards.** Create your own deck of cards, and include on each one a favorite motivational quotation to help you stay positive and build creative confidence. Read one in the morning before you head out to help you start the day on the right note.

• **Fill a box of secrets.** Assemble a box and fill it with your artful goals and places your muse wants to travel to. Each time you achieve a goal, replace it with a new one and add some glitter for extra sparkle.

ART ON THE GO

PICTURE THIS:
ADDING PHOTOGRAPHIC ELEMENTS

by Seth Apter

Taking pictures is a time-honored traveler's activity, and the photographs you take on your journeys can greatly enrich your art once you've arrived home. Unlike the nontraditional materials I use in my work, a camera can travel with me, ready to capture inspiration when I'm on the go, recording life as it happens.

I'm drawn to mixed-media art, in part because by definition it provides me with infinite ways to express myself. I can use any material I choose, from traditional art materials such as paint, gesso, and ink, to nontraditional materials such as found rusty objects, duct tape, and a vintage optical camera lens. I am limited only by my own creativity and imagination.

The same can be said about photography. Nothing is off-limits; anything and everything can be seen through the viewfinder and captured in a split second. One day it might be a portrait of a person in my life; the next day, it may be a detail of a weathered and peeling wall. In both cases, the photograph becomes tangible evidence of my own inner creative world and is a direct expression of me. And one of the best things about a camera is that it's portable!

In my mind, there is a natural pairing between photography and mixed-media art. If you start with an artwork, think of a photograph as an element at your disposal to add another layer to your piece. If you begin with a photograph, realize that every art technique available to you can be employed to enhance your picture. Whether you're adding a photographic element to your art or taking an artful approach to your photograph, creative inspiration is at your fingertips.

I usually integrate photography into my artwork in one of several ways. Because I am so inspired by texture and patina, I'm always on the lookout for distressed surfaces to photograph: walls, fences, objects, billboards, buildings, etc. These become a background layer for my artwork. Printing photos onto different types of paper, such as watercolor paper, maps, or pages of text, creates wonderful substrates to build on. I also often add small details from photographs to artwork in progress to capture a certain feeling, create an additional layer, or add a needed color. In all cases, I alter the image by hand as well.

Overall, using photography in my art gives me the freedom to further enhance my vision. It serves as another tool to express my ideas and to thoroughly personalize my work. It enables me to create something that is uniquely my own. It allows me to create when I travel. Art and photography: It's a match made in heaven.

Top: Seth Apter, *Reasons.* 5" × 7½" (12.5 × 19 cm). Mixed-media collage.

Bottom: Seth Apter, *Picture This.* 7" × 10" (18 × 25.5 cm). Altered-photo collage.

THE PAINT-UNDER TECHNIQUE

By taking Lisa Bebi's paint-over technique (page 113) and going backward, you can achieve a painterly look. Begin with a prepared background and use your own photograph for this project to create unique and personal art. The key to this look is a loose touch with the brush; lay down hints of color and don't blend them too much. By working quickly and adding details with a fast and easy transfer method, you can save a lot of time and still create meaningful and beautiful art.

MATERIALS

- Black-and-white photograph (digital or actual) with an image of a person
- Transparencies for inkjet printers
- Canvas substrate with prepared background
- Graphite pencil
- Fluid or heavy-body acrylic paints in skin tones and additional colors as desired
- Hand sanitizer
- White gel pen or other writing instruments
- Vintage paper scraps such as torn book pages and other text
- Soft gel medium
- Water-soluble crayons

TOOLS

- Inkjet printer
- Scissors
- Paintbrushes
- Sponge brush
- Bone folder

Pam Carriker, *Heart Full of Wisdom*. 8" × 10" (20.5 × 25.5 cm). Acrylic paint and mixed media on canvas.

FIG. 1   FIG. 2   FIG. 3

1 Using an inkjet printer, copy or print a black-and-white photo (alter a color photograph in a photo-editing program if desired) with a clearly defined image of a person onto a transparency. Size the image to fit onto your prepared canvas. With scissors, trim the image closely and lay it on the canvas, tracing around the outside edge with a graphite pencil. Remove the image **(Figure 1)**.

2 Fill in the traced area with a wash of one part water and one part acrylic paint in skin tone **(Figure 2)**.

3 Reinforce the face area with a second coat of paint. Mark basic facial features with graphite pencil, not using too much detail; just mark the placement of the eyes, nose, and mouth **(Figure 3)**.

4 Mix a darker skin tone. With a painterly stroke, loosely shade the eyes, nose, mouth, and chin areas. Blend the paint as you go, adding some darker and lighter tones. Do this quickly and do not overthink this step. Add some lighter dabs of paint to the

cheek, forehead, nose, and chin areas, wherever you want highlights. Add washes of color to clothes to help define them **(Figure 4)**.

5 Lay the transparency, ink side down, on top of the painted face and move the image around until you're happy with the look. Make a couple of marks with a pencil to indicate where the transparency will go **(Figure 5)**.

6 Using a sponge brush, apply hand sanitizer or gel medium to only the facial features on the transparency. Immediately lay the transparency on the background and gently pat to ensure proper adhesion. Use a bone folder to burnish the photo and finish the transfer process. Let the work sit for a few minutes and then gently peel back the transparency and check that the image has transferred. If it hasn't, add more hand sanitizer and repeat the process. Lift off the transparency and let the transfer dry completely **(Figure 6)**.

7 Add color to the hair on the transferred image.

FIG. 4

FIG. 5

8 Add painterly brushstrokes to the face on the transferred image to completely tie in the transfer details with the painted portion. Resketch any lost details with a graphite pencil. Add journaling with a white gel pen, adhere the vintage text with gel medium, and add water-soluble crayon or paint to the background as desired.

FIG. 6

TIP: MAKE MULTIPLES

Print images for future collages all in one sitting at the computer. This saves you from running back and forth (up and down the stairs in my case) from your art desk to the computer.
—Nancy Lefko

SEVEN-DAY JOURNAL
DAY 6: YOUR TWO CENTS

Adding your voice to the page is the most important part of journaling. It can also be intimidating, but it's the perfect take-along project when traveling—what better time to write down what's going on in your life? Some pages pack a punch with a few simple words and others have ramblings that take up the entire page. Some follow lines, while others are random. Consider it creative writing!

MATERIALS

- Seven-Day Journal pages with prepared backgrounds (page 26)
- Woodless graphite pencil
- Ultra-fine permanent marker
- White gel pen

TOOLS

- Eraser
- Ruler

There are no specific steps to this project except to add writing to journal pages in any way that strikes your fancy! Do a practice page using different types of writing, experimenting with different pens. Here are some lettering prompts to try:

- Draw wavy lines and write following the wave pattern.
- Alternate upper- and lowercase letters and fill the holes in the letters with white or another color.
- Draw a pattern lightly in pencil and fit words into it by varying the letter size.
- Write multi-directionally by marking off segments on your page and writing in a different direction in each segment.
- Use just a few words to convey your meaning, giving them added impact by outlining and weighting one side with a thicker line.

DON'T KNOW WHAT TO WRITE?

If you're not sure what to write, look for prompts and inspiration all around you. For example, crossword and word search puzzles make great additions to your journal page. Use rough drafts from articles or other things you've written. A to-do or grocery list is great journal fodder. The menu for a special or even everyday meal becomes "food for thought." Use snippets from children's homework. Look around your house for newspapers, magazines, newsletters, anything with text. Use words from a song, poetry, quotations, something the kids said, a funny bumper sticker, or even that advertising jingle you can't get out of your head.

Once you have an assortment of notes and ideas, follow these steps:

1 Quickly look through and tear out any words or phrases that jump out at you. Don't dwell on this too much; act on your gut instinct.

2 Randomly glue the words and phrases into your art journal using soft gel medium. Apply it to the back of the paper and then add a little to the journal page where the words will be glued. Use a paintbrush to work out any air bubbles as you apply gel medium to the top of the text. When dry, the medium will seal the text, allowing you to paint over it without smearing the ink.

3 Don't throw out extra text or word prompts; store them in a drawer or container to pull out at any time.

Pam Carriker, *Seven-Day Journal.* 8" × 8" (20.5 × 20.5 cm) closed. Handmade journal with mixed-media pages.

CHAPTER 7

RECLAIM YOUR CREATIVE TIME

ART AT THE SPEED OF LIFE

With a new focus on reclaiming your art time, you can now plan your strategy for making more art in the midst of a busy life. Without a plan in place, it's hard to see your dreams become reality. You need very little in the way of supplies to be creative; a simple piece of paper and a pencil will do. But you do need a few moments to indulge your creative spirit. The moment has come to reclaim your creative time! Take a few moments every now and then to reflect on where you've been and to look forward to the future and all that it holds for you, making sure your creative life is heading in the direction of your art's desires.

With an eye turned inward as you reflect on where you want your art life to go, it's the perfect time to work on a self portrait. This chapter's *Artist Spotlight* project by Paulette Insall teaches you her techniques for creating beautiful faces. In my *Speed of Life* version, I show how to create a fast and easy self-portrait using soft pastels (which require no drying time) on a prepared background. Finally, as you finish the *Seven-Day Journal* project, you'll have a visual aide to encourage you on your artful journey.

THE MOMENT HAS COME TO RECLAIM YOUR CREATIVE TIME!

Art Credits: page 143

YOUR LIFE AS ART

If your life were a piece of art, you would now have your substrate chosen, prepped, and with the background painted. You now need to complete the picture, to become a work of art. What will you look like? How will you get there? See who you can be, then be who you can be.

- **Prep your substrate.** Every great piece of art starts with a clean slate and proper preparation. Failure to do this step may lead to problems down the road. Take a moment and prepare yourself both mentally and physically. Live in the creative moment, clearing your mind and work space of clutter that can hinder the creative process.

- **Gather your tools.** You can't create a painting without paint, and you won't be successful at finding time to create without the appropriate tools either. Time is a tool, probably the most valuable one you have. Time truly is a gift we each are given freely. Everyone has the same amount, so embrace it and use it to your advantage.

- **Finish what you start.** Few things are more discouraging than looking at piles of projects left neglected and unfinished. Completing the smallest thing gives more satisfaction than the grandest plan that is left undone. You are a work of art, and your creative journey will be finished piece by piece as you change and grow daily. You'll leave a trail of finished work as stepping-stones for others to walk on as you create new ones to lie in front of your own feet. These are gifts we give to each other: inspiration, encouragement, hope, and sharing our journey with those around us.

Pam Carriker, *Self Examination*. 7" × 11" × 8" (18 × 28 × 20.5 cm). Wig form, plaster strips, collage, and acrylic paint.

BUILDING BLOCKS

As far back as I can remember, my family members have said, "I don't know where you get your artistic ability," as they scratched their heads in bewilderment looking at something I'd made. As I grow older I'm more aware of the creative talents that everyone in my family has, and I realize that what sets me apart from them also ties us together.

My grandfathers and my great-grandfather had a knack for assemblage and a vision for collecting and putting things together. Real working cannons created on a lathe, silverware trays crafted from wood, objects created from vintage kitchen pieces turned into things I still use today, such as my lovely sewing stool. My dad also shares this vision, seeing potential in discarded items as an antiques dealer.

My grandmothers influenced me in the domestic arts, with my maternal grandma patiently teaching my sister and me how to embroider lovely French knots. My mother taught me the importance and pleasure of keeping a nice home and turning something simple into a favorite family meal. She created works of love fashioned from material in the dresses my sister and I wore. Even my creative stepmother has encouraged me and shaped my life.

INSIDE YOU THERE'S AN ARTIST YOU DON'T KNOW ABOUT . . .
—RUMI

Pay attention to where your creativity comes from and build on that foundation. Spend time exploring the creative talents of your family. Creativity isn't limited to a brush and some paint; it can manifest in many ways. Look to your past to help you see where you're heading on your own path to your creative life.

My art has taken me in a different direction, but the building blocks my family laid were crucial to my artistic journey. They may won-

> LOOK TO YOUR PAST TO HELP YOU SEE WHERE YOU'RE HEADING ON YOUR OWN PATH TO YOUR CREATIVE LIFE.

der where my artistic bent came from, but I know it trickled down from all of them. Being creative is a state of being. It isn't just about talent—it's a mindset that allows your desire to create to become a reality.

CONTEMPORARY

EXPRESSIONIST PORTRAIT

by Paulette Insall

I created this project after being in a state of flux artistically and resisting it. Instead of painting the way I was longing to, I tried to paint the way I had been for years. So I stopped painting altogether for a while and focused on other things. Eventually, I realized that this, too, was part of my growth process. Once the walls of resistance came down, I was finally ready to move forward. I know that I'm not done growing yet, but instead of being afraid, I'm excited to see what's next!

MATERIALS

- Fluid acrylic paints: titanium white, zinc white, and several colors of your choice
- Sheet of 140-pound cold press watercolor paper
- Soft graphite pencil
- Spray varnish

TOOLS

- Soft rubber brayer
- Palette
- Paintbrushes, including small and medium flat brushes, medium fan brush, small filbert brush
- Spray bottle for water
- Blending stump

Paulette Insall, *Contemporary Expressionist Portrait.*
8" × 8" (20.5 × 20.5 cm). Mixed media.

FIG. 1   FIG. 2   FIG. 3

1 Using acrylic paints, paint an abstract background on the sheet of watercolor paper. Just drizzle one color at a time onto your paper and randomly roll your brayer over it until the paint will no longer move around the paper. Apply several layers of different colors. Work quickly so that some of the colors mix (**Figure 1**).

2 Pour fluid acrylics onto a palette. Roll the brayer over it to pick up the paint and apply it randomly to the painting. Repeat with several colors.

3 Paint out some areas of the background using a flat brush to apply paint randomly. Lay down solid patches of color on top of the busy background created in the previous steps, creating quiet areas in the background.

4 Splatter paint diluted with water over a few areas by holding a paint-filled fan brush over the painting and tapping it with the end of another paintbrush or a pencil.

5 Sketch a portrait with a soft graphite pencil onto your finished background. Try looking for facial features in the background (**Figure 2**).

6 Choose colors to paint your portrait. They don't have to be skin tones. Try using colors similar to the background (**Figure 3**).

7 Use a filbert brush to paint skin areas. Working quickly, paint in one of the shadow areas with a thin layer of your darkest or most intense paint color (I used cobalt teal). Then paint a thin layer of your main skin color (I used nickel azo gold mixed with titanium white). Blend the two colors by wiping your brush over the edges of each color where they meet with a soft back-and-forth motion. You can also add a third color to accent some areas of the face (I used hansa yellow medium). As you paint, lightly mist the paints on your palette periodically to keep your paints wet. Just one or two sprays will keep them moist without diluting them. Continue this process all around the face and neck until all of the skin areas are filled in with color. Work only in a small area at a time because thinly applied fluid acrylics dry very quickly.

FIG. 4

FIG. 5

Be sure to leave some areas where bits of the background show through.

8 Using titanium white paint and a small flat brush, apply a thin layer to the bridge of the nose and blend outward with a clean filbert brush until you no longer see a line of the newly applied paint. Continue this process on the forehead, chin, and one side of the neck to bring these areas forward and add some dimension to the face (**Figure 4**).

9 Add a few thin layers of zinc white to the whites of the eyes. Let dry between layers.

10 Paint the iris of the eyes using a color from your background. Make a few shades and tints of the eye color by adding a complementary color or a tiny bit of black for shades and white for tints to your chosen eye color. Starting out with the darkest color and graduating to the lightest, layer your colors onto the iris of the eyes. Let dry between layers. Focus the lightest tint on one side of the iris to show reflected light from your perceived light source. Paint the lips in a similar fashion.

11 For the hair, focus the darkest shade on the edges and the lightest tint in the middle. Add a few strands of the darkest shade on top of the lighter areas to create a little more interest. Apply paint layers thinly so that the background shows through the hair areas.

12 For the clothing, draw connecting abstract shapes and fill in each with a different color of fluid acrylic paint. While the paint is still wet, apply a small amount of titanium white in some areas and mix it with the still-wet paint, blending as you go along (**Figure 5**).

13 Apply paint layers thinly to your secondary elements, letting it dry between layers.

14 Loosely outline all edges of the portrait and other elements with a soft graphite pencil. Smudge the lines with a blending stump. You can also apply graphite or charcoal to shadow areas with your blending stump to define them a little more.

15 After the painting has dried for several days and the paints have cured, use a spray varnish to seal and protect your finished painting. Follow the directions on the label and use in a well-ventilated area.

a
self portrait
is a reflection
of the inner self
that sometimes
surprises
the
painter
more than the
viewer

PASTEL
SELF-PORTRAIT

The idea of creating a portrait can seem a little intimidating, but by simplifying the process and using an easy-to-blend medium such as pastels in pans, it's really quite simple. Keep in mind that this is a representation of you, not an exact replica. Use a copy of a photo to create a simplified sketch. Pastels in pan form (I use PanPastel brand) allow you to work fast and blend colors easily with no drying time or mess to create a lovely portrait.

MATERIALS

- Colored pencil in a color that will show up well on the photocopy
- Black-and-white photocopy of a photo of yourself
- Woodless graphite pencil
- Prepared background, 9" × 12" (23 × 30.5 cm)
- Clear gesso
- Acrylic paints in colors of your choice
- Pastels (I prefer PanPastel brand in pans): burnt sienna tint, raw umber, Payne's gray, white, permanent red tint, additional colors of your choice
- White gel pen
- Water-soluble crayons
- Spray fixative
- Satin-finish polymer varnish

TOOLS

- Bone folder
- Paintbrushes including ¾" (2 cm) flat
- Assorted stamps and texture tools such as sequin waste or a sea sponge
- If using pastels in pans, a palette knife and sponge applicator (I use Sofft Tools For PanPastels No. 4 Point Palette Knife and Mini Applicator)
- Sponge brush

Pam Carriker, *Self-Portrait*. 9" × 12" (23 × 30.5 cm). Pastel and acrylic on board.

FIG. 1   FIG. 2   FIG. 3

1 With a colored pencil, trace over the basic features on the photocopy of your face and adjust to get a simple, bare-bones sketch. Transfer your sketch to your prepared background by turning it over and coloring graphite pencil onto the back of the copy. Position the sketch on the substrate, graphite side down, and burnish with a bone folder to transfer the graphite pencil to the prepared background. You can further adjust the sketch with graphite pencil directly on the background as needed (**Figure 1**).

2 Paint a coat of clear gesso over the sketch to provide some tooth for the pastels to adhere to. Using an X brushstroke, crisscross back and forth randomly to create texture. Let dry (**Figure 2**).

3 Add additional paint, stamping, journaling, and textural elements to the background as desired (**Figure 3**).

4 Use a palette knife to apply a base color (I used burnt sienna tint) for the skin (**Figure 4**). (If using the Sofft Tool knife, gently swipe across the pan two

or three times and then use a gentle touch to apply to the face area using a patting, painterly stroke.)

5 Try not to lose the outlines of the face details; if needed, touch up with a graphite pencil in between pastel applications. Add an additional layer of base coat color for good coverage.

6 Using a small sponge applicator or the Sofft Tool applicator, begin shading. Pat once on burnt sienna tint and once on raw umber. Use painterly strokes, gently blending to the background color to shade facial details. The more you pat and work the colors, the more they blend. Resketch face details as needed (**Figure 5**).

7 Deepen the shaded areas further using straight raw umber, this time going over the pencil marks to blend them in a bit. Shade the upper lip and the bottom of the lower lip with raw umber (**Figure 6**).

8 Shade the darkest areas with just a touch of Payne's gray. Highlight details with white pastel,

FIG. 4

FIG. 5

FIG. 6

using it to fill in the eyes as well. Use the white gel pen to add highlights to the eyes. Color in the iris of the eye with the color of your choice **(Figure 7)**.

9 Use the graphite pencil to add eye details and to define the lip area a bit. Use pastel in permanent red tint to add a touch of color to the cheeks and lips. Sketch the clothing and color with the water-soluble crayons, activating the crayon with a wet brush. Use water-soluble crayons to color the hair, activating it with a wet brush. Define the brows with graphite pencil.

10 To finish, spray several light coats of fixative, letting each coat dry in between, and then finish with a coat of polymer varnish, applied with a sponge brush, if desired.

FIG. 7

SEVEN-DAY JOURNAL
DAY 7: ADDING YOU TO THE MIX

By now, your journal is close to completion. It documents your journey to becoming more focused and reflects the goals you have as an artist. In it you now have many of the techniques from this book, as well as things you brought to it from your own arsenal of creativity. There is one thing left that will make this journal truly about your journey: a self-portrait on the front cover and a list of your artistic goals on the back. Here is a simple way to add these personal touches to your journal.

THE FRONT COVER:
A SIMPLE SELF-PORTRAIT

MATERIALS

- A black-and-white photocopy of a photo of yourself
- Soft gel medium
- Seven-Day Journal (page 26)
- Gesso
- Woodless graphite pencil
- White charcoal

TOOLS

- Scissors or X-acto knife
- Paintbrush
- Blending stump

1 With scissors or an X-acto knife, cut around the image of yourself on the photocopy.

2 Using a paintbrush, apply soft gel medium to the photocopy and adhere it to the journal cover. Let dry thoroughly.

3 Apply a mix of one part gesso and one part water to the picture and wipe off the excess so you can still see the shadows of the photocopy showing through a bit. Let this dry.

4 Use the woodless graphite pencil to draw the facial features back in.

5 With the blending stump, gently rub the pencil around the shaded areas, following the shading in the photo.

6 Add some white highlights with the white charcoal.

THE BACK COVER:
REFLECT

MATERIALS

- Pens, assorted
- Words clipped from old book pages
- Soft gel medium
- Seven-Day Journal (page 26)
- Collage images
- Graphite pencil
- Assorted acrylic paints (optional)
- Library card with paper sleeve

TOOLS

- Scissors
- Paintbrush

1 Add some words to the back cover of your journal that are descriptive of how you see yourself. Write them by hand or cut words from text with scissors and glue them down with soft gel medium, using a paintbrush to apply the medium to the back of the text and over the text after it has been put in place.

2 Add some images that speak to you, cutting them out with scissors and gluing them down with soft gel medium as in step 1.

3 Write some thoughts about who you are in pencil. If you don't want these readable, cover them over with a wash of paint diluted with water so they're barely visible.

4 List goals for your creative journey on a library card and attach a paper sleeve for the card to the back cover of the journal with soft gel medium.

Pam Carriker, *Seven-Day Journal*. 8" × 8" (20.5 × 20.5 cm) closed. Handmade journal with mixed-media pages.

DECLARATION OF RECLAMATION

Reclaim Creative Time

Set Goals and Write Them Down

Focus on Your Favorite Media and Techniques

Economize and Downsize to Regain Control

Organize and Prioritize Time and Supplies

Tear this page out and hang it where you can see it!

GET READY, GET SET, GO!

So you're motivated and full of ideas and inspiration for new projects and techniques you want to try, and maybe you're actually thinking about tidying up your art space. The next step is to do it! Start small to make sure you'll succeed. It's the act of doing rather than wishing that makes all the difference.

As you take the first step toward making time to create, you're telling yourself that it's okay. You don't need to feel guilty because you love art and creating is so deliciously fun it feels like you're doing something illegal. Not everything that's fun is bad for you! And when you share what you've done with others, they'll be inspired to continue the cycle. Exploring your creative side will lead you to becoming the person you were meant to be.

Sometimes life will make it impossible to even pick up a brush. That's no reason to give up! Those are the days you renew your promise to make time for art. Time is constant. The clock starts over every day. We all have the same twenty-four hours in a day no matter who we are or where we come from, and it's up to each of us to use it to the fullest. "I just do it," says my friend Suzan Buckner when people ask her how she creates so much art. It really is as simple as that. It's a decision that you make and remake daily, even hourly. At times you may have to let something else go, and that's okay, too.

Some days you'll make great strides and see growth and other days the smallest of baby steps is all that you can manage. It's all good. Even the smallest step brings you closer to living *Art at the Speed of Life*!

Pam Carriker, *Together*.
6" × 12" (15 × 30.5 cm).
Mixed-media collage
painting using Brandie
Butcher-Isley's techniques.

I AM NOW RICH IN FRUITFUL IDEAS
AND I MUST PRODUCE MY WORK.
—AMEDEO MODIGLIANI

ABOUT THE CONTRIBUTORS

Seth Apter

thealteredpage.blogspot.com

Seth Apter is a mixed-media artist and photographer from New York who focuses primarily on works on paper, book arts, and textural assemblage. His artwork is highly textured and distressed, using layers of paper, paint, ink, text, and found objects. Seth's work has been widely exhibited and published. He has developed and hosted several collaborative projects including The Pulse, an ongoing artist survey, and the Disintegration Collaboration.
See pages 89, 94, 95–97, 106, 116, 117.

Lisa Bebi

lisabebi.blogspot.com

Candid snapshots inspire Lisa Bebi. She earned a degree in fine art with an emphasis in painting and printmaking at San Diego State University and studied commercial art lettering and painting at the College of Fine Art, London University. Lisa is a frequent contributor and an artist-on-call for *Somerset Studio* magazines. Lisa's work is continually on display in the Escondido Municipal Gallery in Escondido, California.
See pages 107, 112, 113, 119, 124, 125.

Julie Bergmann

juliebergmann.typepad.com

Julie Bergmann has been an artist all of her life, recently focusing on mixed media, altered art, and artist trading cards. Through experimentation, Julie discovered a love for papier-mâché and began to use fine pulp products in her work.
See pages 13, 33.

Laurie Blau-Marshall

loudlife-laurieblaumarshall.blogspot.com

Laurie Blau-Marshall is a painter, jewelry artist, and mixed-media artist. She has sold and shown her work throughout the northwest United States, has had her artwork in various publications, and her jewelry art worn in a television movie. She's living the life of her dreams with her husband and beautiful daughter in the Seattle area.
See pages 68, 72, 73.

Suzi Blu

alovelydream.com

Suzi Blu is an inspirational and motivational artist and teacher who instructs aspiring artists through her online school, Les Petit Academy. Known for her whimsical portraits, she makes pretty art in her gypsy wagon with her best friend Gigi, and intends to prove to you that you are an artist whether you like it or not!
See pages 9, 12, 106, 107, 111.

Suzan Buckner

suzanbuckner.com

Suzan Buckner is a self-taught Alabama folk-art and mixed-media artist. Suzan has been published in many art-journaling publications and has taught art journaling classes at the Huntsville Art League. She also paints and makes art dolls, assemblage, and collages.
See pages 29, 34, 35, 85, 124, 139.

Brandie Butcher-Isley

littlepiecesofart.com

Brandie Butcher-Isley is a self-taught mixed-media artist in West Des Moines, Iowa. Her art grew from photographs of family relatives. Today, Brandie uses discarded photographs of individuals discovered at estate sales and antique stores. She creates fictional stories for the people in these photographs with layers of art media to breathe life back into those whose photographic records have been misplaced or forgotten.
See pages 28, 29, 36–39, 88.

Cate Coulacos Prato

clothpaperscissors.com

Cate Coulacos Prato is a writer, editor, and amateur home decorator. She is the author of *Mixed-Media Self-Portraits: Inspiration & Techniques* (Interweave, 2008). She brakes for vintage linens and the occasional interesting table.
See pages 32–33.

Dawn Edmonson

the-feathered-nest.blogspot.com

Dawn Edmonson creates one-of-a-kind artwork and sells it in her online shop. She is drawn to all things old and uses small antique trinkets in her artwork. Dawn's work has been published in more than a dozen artist magazines. She loves sharing what she learns and creates through her blog and her tutorials. Dawn is married with five sons and is grandmother to a little girl.
See pages 48, 53.

Christy Hydeck

alwayschrysti.com

Christy Hydeck is an artist, writer, and photographer whose work is influenced by her love of animals, children, whimsy, and all things odd. She is an avid collector of words, a dreamer, a lover of nature, and a big believer in miracles. Christy immerses herself in the wondrous magic of creativity. She aspires to share her vision for finding the extraordinary in the ordinary through tutorials and personal instruction.
See pages 8, 9, 14–18, 80–81, 125.

Paulette Insall

pauletteinsall.com

Paulette Insall is a painter who creates many-layered visual narratives inspired by her faith in God, scripture, music, and life. Her work focuses on spiritual themes meant to up-lift and inspire the viewer. Paulette offers online mixed-media painting classes through her blog and DVD workshops on her website. Paulette's classes are structured to encourage students to explore and trust their creative voices and listen to their intuition. Paulette lives outside of Portland, Oregon, with her husband and son.
See pages 48, 60, 61, 125, 128–131.

Lisa Kettell

moonfairesworld.com

Lisa Kettell, based in New Jersey, works in a number of artistic media. Her work is fueled by her love of history, her world travels, and her imagination. She shares her creativity through *The Faerie Zine*, dedicated to the unlimited possibilities in the world of art. Lisa's artwork has been widely published, and she has contributed to a variety of design teams. She teaches workshops and is licensing a new line of products.
See pages 6, 106, 115.

Nancy Lefko

mycollageart.com

Nancy Lefko creates mixed-media collage art. A former elementary school teacher, she brought her love of art into the classroom. Today, Nancy teaches online workshops and sells her artwork. Nancy's artwork has been published in *Cloth Paper Scissors*, *Art Journaling by Somerset*, *Somerset Studio Gallery*, and *Somerset Studio* magazines. Nancy lives in Peterborough, New Hampshire, with her husband and three sons.
See pages 68, 78, 79, 121.

Jodi Ohl

sweetrepeats.blogspot.com

Jodi Ohl is a self-taught mixed-media artist in Aberdeen, North Carolina. Her work is known for its delightful whimsical subjects, often bold and colorful. She has published articles in *Cloth Paper Scissors* magazine, and participated in the collaborative Sisterhood of the Traveling Canvas project for Somerset Studios. When she is not working at her job in banking, she conducts mixed-media workshops in North Carolina and online at creativeworkshops.ning.com.
See pages 8, 18, 92, 93.

Sue Pelletier

suepelletierlaughpaint.com

Words, whimsy, and humor inspire Sue Pelletier's artwork. Sue loves flea markets and yard sales and finding mismatched pieces to incorporate into her art. Sue has long been an elementary school art teacher in Dover, Massachusetts, and the spontaneity in children's art inspires her. Her work has been featured in *Cloth Paper Scissors* magazine.
See pages 49, 56, 57, 124.

Gail Schmidt

shabbycottagestudio.com

Gail Schmidt is a mixed-media artist living in a 1920s farmhouse cottage in the mountains of Tennessee with her husband (aka Mr. Shabby), dog, and cat, on an acre of land. After fifteen years as a painter, Gail now immerses herself in vintage-inspired mixed-media and digital collage. She runs an online store and an online workshop community. Gail's work has been published in Somerset's *Digital Studio*.
See pages 49, 55.

Sharon Tomlinson

allnorahsart.blogspot.com

Sharon Tomlinson is a self-taught artist living in Marlin, Texas. She can be found at her desk job daydreaming about her next art project in her studio at home. She creates mixed-media art and collage on canvas, altered books, and journals. Sharon's art and writing can be found in numerous art publications, and she teaches online workshops.
See pages 88, 89, 98, 99.

TwoCoolTexans

redhead7.blogspot.com
alishafredrickson.blogspot.com

Mother and daughter Glenda Bailey and Alisha Fredrickson are self-taught mixed-media artists who work individually and collaboratively. Glenda is a widely published artist who works in fabric, acrylics, collage, encaustic, and felt, and teaches classes on craftedu.com. Alisha, whose work has been featured on Home and Garden Television, is a mother of two who finds that art keeps her sane. Glenda and Alisha live in Texas.
See pages 28, 29, 40, 41, 69, 74–77.

RESOURCES

MIXED-MEDIA SUPPLIES

Activa Products
activaproducts.com
Makers of Celluclay.

Golden Paints
goldenpaints.com
Golden offers a wide range of paints, gels, and mediums.

Interweave
interweavestore.com
Mixed-media supplies.

Jacquard Products
jacquardproducts.com
Fabric paints and textile art supplies, including Lumiere paints.

Judikins
judikins.com
Rubber stamps and accessories; Judikins Diamond Glaze.

Matisse Derivan
matissederivan.com
Art supplies, including Derivan Liquid Pencil.

PanPastel Colors
panpastel.com
Soft artist's painting pastels in pans.

Ranger Ink & Innovative Craft Products
collageartist.com/claudine_hellmuth_studio.htm
Ranger offers Claudine Hellmuth Studio products.

Sofft Tools
sofftart.com
Tools for arts and crafts, including knives, sponges, and applicators.

Tsukineko
tsukineko.com
Pigment, dye, and craft inks for stamping, including StazOn inks.

Uniball
uniball-na.com
Makers of the Signo white gel pen.

INTERNET INSPIRATION

Cloth Paper Scissors
clothpaperscissors.com
The online community of *Cloth Paper Scissors* magazine.

Creative Therapy
creativetherapy.wordpress.com
An online community about using art to heal.

Creative Workshops
creativeworkshops.ning.com
Online classes in mixed-media techniques.

Crescendoh
crescendoh.com
Jenny Doh's mixed-media creative community.

I Love To Create Blog
ilovetocreateblog.blogspot.com
Daily inspiration.

Violette's Creative Juice
violette.ca
Creative inspiration.

RECOMMENDED READING

Cole, Shona. *The Artistic Mother: A Practical Guide for Fitting Creativity into Your Life.* North Light Books, 2010.

Cozen, Chris. *Altered Surfaces: Using Acrylic Paints With Gels, Mediums, Grounds & Pastes.* Design Originals, 2008.

Hellmuth, Claudine. *Collage Discovery Workshop.* North Light Books, 2003.

Prato, Cate Coulacos. *Mixed-Media Self-Portraits: Inspiration & Techniques.* Interweave, 2008.

Trout, Diana. *Journal Spilling: Mixed-Media Techniques for Free Expression.* North Light Books, 2010.

ADDITIONAL ART CREDITS

All artwork is mixed media.

Page 6, clockwise from left: Pam Carriker, *Together*, 12" × 6" (30.5 × 15 cm); Lisa Kettell, *A Creative Journey*, 6" × 9" (15 × 23 cm) closed; Pam Carriker, *Toilette Papier Mâché*, 8" × 12" (20.5 × 30.5 cm).

Page 7: Pam Carriker, *Seven-Day Journal*, 8" × 8" (20.5 × 20.5 cm).

Page 8, from left: Jodi Ohl, *New Beginning*, 6" × 12" (15 × 30.5 cm); Christy Hydeck, *A Garden of Beautiful Ideas*, 16" × 20" (40.5 × 51 cm).

Page 9, clockwise from left: Suzi Blu, *A Lovely Dream*, 7" × 9" (18 × 23 cm) closed; Christy Hydeck, work in progress, 8" × 10" (20.5 × 25.5 cm); Pam Carriker, *A Change of Heart*, 8" × 8" (20.5 × 20.5 cm).

Page 28, clockwise from left: Pam Carriker, *Never Enough*, 8" × 8" (20.5 × 20.5 cm); Brandie Butcher-Isley, *Heartfelt Collage*, 5" × 7" (12.5 × 18 cm); Alisha Fredrickson, *Mother and Child*, 4" × 4" (10 × 10 cm).

Page 29, from left: Suzan Buckner, *Three Men*, 12" × 12" (30.5 × 30.5 cm); Glenda Bailey, *Butterflies and Roses*, 6" × 8" (15 × 20.5 cm).

Page 48, clockwise from left: Paulette Insall, *Lead Me*, 8" × 10" (20.5 × 25.5 cm); Dawn Edmonson, *Love's Whisper*, 9½" (24 cm) diameter; Dawn Edmonson, *Beekeeper*, 4½" × 6" (11.5 × 15 cm).

Page 49, from left: Sue Pelletier, *100 Dresses Series*, 12" × 12" (30.5 × 30.5 cm); Gail Schmidt, *Altered Child's Board Book*, 5" × 6½" (12.5 × 16.5 cm).

Page 68, clockwise from left: Pam Carriker, *My Eyes Make Pictures . . .*, 8" × 8" (20.5 × 20.5 cm); Laurie Blau-Marshall, *To Use, To Feel, To Be*, 4" × 12" (10 × 30.5 cm); Nancy Lefko, *Living the Artful Life*, 8" × 10" (20.5 × 25.5 cm).

Page 69, from top: Pam Carriker, *Together*, 12" × 6" (30.5 × 15 cm); Glenda Bailey, *A Token of Remembrance*, 6" × 6" (15 × 15 cm).

Page 88, clockwise from left: Sharon Tomlinson, *From the Desk of . . .*, 5" × 5" (12.5 × 12.5 cm); Brandie Butcher-Isley, *Your Stories*, 6" × 12" (15 × 30.5 cm); Brandie Butcher-Isley, *Where Have You Been?*, 11" × 15" (28 × 38 cm).

Page 89: Sharon Tomlinson, *Glory*, 8" × 10" (20.5 × 25.5 cm).

Page 106, clockwise from left: Suzi Blu, *I Am An Artist*, 12" × 6" (30.5 × 15 cm); Seth Apter, *An Object Found*, 4½" × 6½" (11.5 × 16.5 cm); Lisa Kettell, *A Creative Journey*, 6" × 9" (15 × 23 cm).

Page 107: Suzi Blu, *Live Big*, 12" × 24" (30.5 × 61 cm).

Page 124, clockwise from left: Sue Pelletier, *Tippy Toes*, 12" × 12" (30.5 × 30.5 cm); Suzan Buckner, *Good Girl*, 9" × 12" (23 × 30.5 cm); Lisa Bebi, *Spring Break*, 8" × 8" (20.5 × 20.5 cm).

Page 125, from top: Christy Hydeck, *Scatter Joy*, 16" × 20" (40.5 × 51 cm); Lisa Bebi, *Three Journals*, each 5½" × 9" (14 × 23 cm).

INDEX

Explore even more

INSPIRATIONAL
MIXED-MEDIA

project ideas with these
imaginative resources
from Interweave

Mixed Mania
Recipes for Delicious
Mixed-Media Creations
*Debbi Crane
and Cheryl Prater*
ISBN 978-1-59668-084-5
$22.95

where mixed-media artists come to play

Clothpaperscissors.com is the online
community where mixed-media artists
come to play and share creative ideas.
Receive expert tip and techniques,
e-newsletters, blogs, forums, videos,
special offers, and more! Join today.

cloth.paper
scissors

The magazine for both beginner and
seasoned artists interested in trying
new techniques and sharing their work
and expertise with a greater audience.
Subscribe at **clothpaperscissors.com**

Art + Quilt
Design Principles
and Creativity
Exercises
Lyric Kinard
ISBN 978-1-59668-106-4
$26.95

Mixed Media Explorations
Blending Paper, Fabric, and
Embellishment to Create
Inspired Designs
Beryl Taylor
ISBN 978-0-9766928-2-9
$27.99

INTERWEAVE
interweave.com